W9-BPS-349

Reclaiming Reluctant Writers

How to encourage students to face their fears and master the essential traits of good writing

KELLIE BUIS

LIBRARY
FRANKLIN PIERCE UNIVERSITY
RINDGE, NH 03461

Pembroke Publishers Limited

Thank you to John, Alena, Jamie, and Zak
who continue to share in my love
of the printed word.

Pembroke Publishers
538 Hood Road
Markham, Ontario, Canada L3R 3K9
www.pembrokepublishers.com

Distributed in the U.S. by Stenhouse Publishers
480 Congress Street
Portland, ME 04101
www.stenhouse.com

© 2007 Pembroke Publishers
All rights reserved.
No part of this publication may be reproduced in any form or by any means electronic or mechanical, including photocopy, recording, or any information, storage or retrieval system, without permission in writing from the publisher.

Every effort has been made to contact copyright holders for permission to reproduce borrowed material. The publishers apologize for any such omissions and will be pleased to rectify them in subsequent reprints of the book.

We acknowledge the financial support of the Government of Canada through the Book Publishing Industry Development Program (BPIDP) for our publishing activities.

We acknowledge the Government of Ontario through the Ontario Media Development Corporation's Ontario Book Initiative.

Library and Archives Canada Cataloguing in Publication

Buis, Kellie
   Reclaiming reluctant writers : how to encourage students to face their fears and master the essential traits of good writers / Kellie Buis.

Includes index.
ISBN 978-1-55138-220-3
   1. English language—Composition and exercises—Study and teaching (Elementary). 2. English language—Composition and exercises—Study and teaching (Secondary). 3. English language—Remedial teaching. I. Title.

LB1631.B7735 2007   372.62'3044   C2007-904162-0

Editor: Kate Revington
Cover Design: John Zehethofer
Typesetting: Jay Tee Graphics Ltd.

Printed and bound in Canada
9 8 7 6 5 4 3 2 1

Contents

Introduction:
The Challenge of Reclaiming Reluctant Writers

THE CHALLENGE

Reluctant Writer . . .

who me . . . write?

anything?
hmmm
how much?
a page . . . ?
hmmmm,

maybe . . .
how about—
blood and guts
or aliens
or . . .
last night's DVD
ok
i'm Done
can i go?

—Kellie Buis

I so admire Adam. Adam stands before a class of fifth graders with a grin from ear to ear and eyes that sparkle. The welted reddish rash that used to routinely crawl up his neck is nowhere to be seen. Confidence exudes from his proud posture as he releases himself from a deep bow at the conclusion of his first-ever student-led writing exhibition. He giggles under a crop of undecidedly brown hair as the last claps from the hugely appreciative audience subside. He puts down a story about his cats as he collects them up into his arms to return them to their carrying case. Adam has done an amazing job of authoring his comical story about life with his pets, complete with a Complaining poem about their antics in the dryer.

As Adam's teacher, I breathe a sigh of relief. Adam remains reclaimed—for the moment—proud and acclaimed as an author whose writing has drenched his peers in tears of laughter. He has shared a side of himself that none of these students is familiar with.

I marvel at the transformation of Adam from reluctant writer to star of his school stage. Much planning and patience have gone into supporting Adam's shift from a reclusive pencil breaker to a willing writer. I look forward to other wonderful stories I know this lovely boy has to share and other luminous moments where he will shine—and his voice will be heard.

Reluctant writers, as Adam once was, need not be lost from our writing programs. We, as classroom teachers, have the capacity and resources to reclaim them as competent writers.

We reclaim them in the sense that we claim back or recover their desire to write once again as they did when they entered school. By the intermediate grades, this willingness to write deteriorates for many students, although most began school with a positive attitude towards composing (Applebee, Langer, and Mullis 1986). Their attitudes change depending on how the teacher makes choices and controls the writing environment. We reclaim our reluctant writers when we create enabling environments where they can repossess choice and control of their writing and thus, their desire to write willingly—and ideally, write willingly and well.

We can support reluctant writers and challenge them in the right proportions, at the right times. We don't have to cajole them or remediate them. We don't have to blame them for lack of success. Rather, we can build on their strengths and teach them what it takes to be authentic writers. If they don't write willingly and well, instead of giving up on them or feeling sorry for ourselves, we can take a deep, hard look at what to do.

Reluctant Writers: Who Are They?

Reluctant writers come in different sizes and shapes, may be male or female, and can be found at most of our schools today. They aren't born reluctant writers and they don't enter school like this; yet, somewhere along the way, they lose heart—they become disillusioned. Sensing they have little power over what they can say and write, they begin to feel marginalized. They become convinced that they have no connections to others, no ability, no voice, no significant role to play. They develop a vivid sense of their limitations and become anxious or even fearful.

In extreme cases, reluctant writers present themselves as uncooperative and oppositional. More often, they appear withdrawn, sleepy, bored, or indifferent. These behaviors, generated out of their growing indifference, fear, or anxiety, often mimic attitudes of ignorance and reluctance. They encounter difficulties as ELL, ESL, low progress, and at-risk students with few options to overcome them. What we observe as banality is largely their apprehension in disguise.

Some reluctant writers, no longer wishing to be regarded for their insights and understandings, minimize their participation as a safeguard. Hoping to remain invisible, they hide their feelings behind bravado or veil them in silence. They become more concerned with the need to shield, rather than share, their ideas. They wear masks to survive. They may be convinced that we know they are failures and need to act the part. They can become hard to like, hard to teach—and probably need us the most.

Reluctant writers may have developed their attitude as a result of unnatural writing conditions experienced. They may have significant learning difficulties, linguistic difficulties, learning disabilities, or English as another language. They may have only minor difficulties, where they are anxious over one aspect of writing process, or not have difficulty coordinating this knowledge, but struggle for a host of personal reasons. They may be physically handicapped or psychologically "stuck" or "defended" students—defended students are unwilling to take direction from an adult they do not trust or have a secure relationship with (Neufeld and Mate 2004).

Reluctant writers, for the specific purposes of our challenge, are any students in Grades 3 to 9 with difficulties coordinating knowledge on a page. Regardless of the cause of the reluctance, we focus on any writers approaching writing tasks in a state of apprehension that diminishes or shuts down their desire to willingly write well. We direct our attention and intervention to any or all of those who need to recover this desire to willingly write.

Identifying Critical Success Factors

Many of the conditions in our classrooms that reduce students to reluctant writers reflect misconceptions about the teaching and learning of writing. We may inadvertently take missteps in how we teach writing because we don't truly understand the nature of it: the functions, writing process, and so on. We sometimes take missteps in our assigning of learning activities and in the way we organize the conditions of learning in our classrooms.

Myths about the nature of writing, and how it is learned and practised, handicap our best efforts to reclaim these students. We may remain "unaware" of the success factors that revive writer engagement—until now.

By systematically examining the myths and realities of the teaching and learning of writing, we can address the critical success factors for each and shift our teaching practice to best support them—or meet the needs they represent. The shifts we make are indeed critical: *critical* meaning important times when the writing conditions could get better or worse quickly. To identify these potential shifts in our teaching practice is to begin to deal with the important times when these conditions could quickly get better or worse for our writers, and allow us to create the stable, enabling environment necessary to reclaim them.

Chapter 1 presents an enabling environment as the overarching critical success factor in reclaiming reluctant writers; it argues that a complementary approach to teaching—one that combines aspects of process writing and explicit genre teaching—be taken.

From there, Chapters 2 through 7 systematically introduce specific factors that are critical to success in meeting specific challenges in nurturing reluctant writers in essential aspects of writing. These ways of giving students care and protection to grow, develop, and thrive as writers are outlined briefly below:

Chapter	Specific Challenge	Critical Success Factor
2	nurturing the discovery and flow of ideas	the need for interesting, fun, experiential writing
3	nurturing fluency	the need for personal writing
4	nurturing style (voice and word choice)	the need for imitation
5	nurturing organization	the need for planning when going public
6	nurturing reflective revising, editing, and publishing	the need for shared responsibility
7	nurturing pride	the need for connecting, talking, and celebrating

Shifting Practice to Promote Engagement

In this resource, each specific challenge and critical success factor, most simply referred to as a need, is matched with a recommended classroom-tested shift in teaching practice and in the design of writing/learning activities. Major shifts:

- *Eyewitness events*, to nurture the discovery and flow of ideas (see Chapter 2)
- *Eyewitness writers' notebooks, free writes*, and *Progress journals*, used in long writing blocks, to nurture writing fluency (see Chapter 3)
- Exemplary *read-alouds* and *write-alouds*, to nurture writers' voices and word choices (see Chapter 4)
- *Eyewitness Organizers*, two-page graphic organizers that promote understanding of genre, to nurture a sense of text organization (see Chapter 5)
- *Peer conferencing*, to nurture the revising, editing, and publishing practices of our reluctant writers (see Chapter 6)
- *Student-led writing exhibitions*, to nurture pride (see Chapter 7)

Questions to Ground Teaching Practice

To fully enable our reluctant writers to write, we need certain conditions in our classrooms. We can't risk making learning to write any more unnatural, awkward, or difficult than these students already find it. Here are questions to ask now—and beyond:

- What myths and realities pertain to working with reluctant writers?
- How can these myths and realities inform our teaching practice?
- What specific challenges do we face in teaching each of the essential traits of writing to reluctant writers?
- What critical success factors pertain to these challenges?
- What shifts in teaching practice would enable our reluctant writers?

If we can address these, then we can reclaim our most reluctant writers.

The poem is an example of free verse, where a writer captures an experience through an economical choice of words not bound to a particular style, rhythmic pattern, or form. Providing free-verse poetry as a choice is one way to help reluctant writers find their voices.

GETTING BETTER

I think
The writing I did myself
was good.
I didn't think that I could do this,
but
I, imagine me,
I did it.
When I finished I felt good.
I was excited, so many people
saw my writing.

I wouldn't mind
doing something like this again.
Much better than I thought
I, imagine me, that I,
did it . . . Yeah,
I wouldn't mind
doing something like this again.
—Adam

1: The Need for Enabling Environments

Kyle and Kevin are writing poetry about the transformation of their mealworms into beetles. Their careful monitoring of the growth and development of these tiny worms over several weeks has had an impact on their respect and regard for the life cycle of the beetle. Their depth of understanding through first-hand witness has made them experts on the subject as evidenced in the ease with which they put words to this conspicuous change in the mealworms' structure. Witnessing metamorphosis, one of the great miracles of life, inspires these writing partners to create some fine free-verse poetry.

BEETLE LIFE

Lifeless
Suit of black armor
Lying on the ground after a deadly fight
No longer a fright

Was
New and anxious
With a soft coat of armor,
And some pristine shiny wings
White brown and eager to try out his advanced body
No longer thinking of his segmented past

He often wishes to take flight
But his home is here
And forever he shall stay . . .

Old and black
Looking for a mate
Day and night

Now
No memory of his larva past
But he knows how to survive in this body
Wings now old and tarnished
Wind beaten and tired
His underbelly red and raw
Legs and antennae also red and raw
He is now more cautious than his larva counterparts

But his life has come to an end
And soon
A new generation
Will come along.

The struggle is not in how to
motivate students to learn. The
struggle is in creating lessons and
classroom environments that focus
and attract students' intrinsic
motivation: thus, increasing the
likelihood students will actively
engage in the learning.
— Spence Rogers, Jim Ludington, and Shari
Graham, *Motivation and Learning*, p. 2

Myth: Writing classrooms are places in which we can expect students to write well, even our most reluctant writers.

Reality: Most classrooms are places we cannot expect writers to write willingly and well. Reluctant writers do not learn to write willingly through direct teaching —quite often that is what has gotten them into difficulty in the first place. Too much teaching and too many restrictions on their choices for writing can cause them to backslide into boredom and lack of interest or concern for their writing. Authentic writing, the kind of writing that real-world, professional authors do, cannot generally be learned through lectures and repetitive isolated writing exercises. Reluctant writers have little motivation to attend to drills and the teaching of spelling and grammar rules; typically, they do not work well when they lack input into what is learned and how it is learned.

Reluctant writers, however, do not learn to write willingly and well through process writing either—quite often that has gotten them into difficulty, as well. Although writers benefit from doing some process-oriented writing that leads them through the same steps as real-life authors and puts value on what they can do as writers, they still do not fully regain control or authority over what they write. Process writing demands that writers take risks, reveal themselves, and push themselves to take in knowledge, use knowledge, and share it. Reluctant writers tend to experience the difficult and challenging aspects of risk taking— revealing themselves and pushing themselves—but few of the wonderful, rewarding aspects of writing. Many of them clearly lack *authority* over their writing process: that is, they lack an ability to manage or control what they write and how they write (including choice of topic and the necessary conditions to enable their writing). They are easily defeated by what it seems they can't do as writers.

Overarching Challenge: Engagement is reduced to its lowest level for *teachers* of reluctant writers when they have no teaching plan of how to meet the diverse, unique needs of these defeated writers. It is our challenge to intervene and provide options beyond what has not already worked for our most reluctant writers. How do we create lessons and classroom environments that focus and attract students' intrinsic motivation? If we can do that, we increase the likelihood of actively engaging students in writing willingly and well.

Personally, I am always ready to
learn, although I do not always like
being taught.
—Winston Churchill

Specific Challenges: Engagement is reduced to its lowest level for *reluctant writers* when they are expected to write in classrooms where they have no authority over their writing. How do we create enabling environments so that we nurture the abilities of our reluctant writers in developing ideas, organization, voice, word choice, sentence fluency, and conventions as competent writers and thus reclaim them? By Grade 3, it is already a case of trying to help some students regain the life interest and engagement that they had as fledgling Grade 1 students.

Meeting the Need

Given that many reluctant writers have not improved their writing within the confines of either a conventional process-oriented Writers' Workshop or a traditional prescriptive and product-centred writing approach, we somehow need to re-conceptualize our teaching approach. We can do so through a comprehensive teaching plan based on writing actions.

Actions, according to Donald Graves (1989, p. 11), "are teaching approaches to try—yourself or with children—that put us 'in motion' with experiments in learning."

We use writing action plans as a series of writing experiences to meet the needs of our reluctant writers. We do *not* use language arts textbooks or workbook exercises to do this, but instead, take our students through three- to six-week action plans designed to restore their willingness to write.

We typically begin these action plans with students participating in experiential learning, or *Eyewitness events*—much as they did in the early primary grades. These events are followed by several days of immersion in studying and imitating a genre through read-alouds and write-alouds. Then, there are several days of collecting and organizing ideas onto paper—planning tools we call *organizers*. These actions are followed by open writing time, or sessions, where writers extend their ideas through drafting, revising, and editing any writing to be published, or choose to do personal, first draft–only writing. These actions are followed by inviting writers to connect with one another, talk, and celebrate what they have learned with an audience—we call these opportunities *student-led exhibitions*.

Writing action plans sustain our writers through the exploration of several genres, perhaps 6 to 12, throughout the year. We want our students to be writing in many genres, such as description, non-fiction inquiries and explorations, and poetry. Some of these will be learned as part of whole-class writing actions and some through private writing. Action plans serve the needs of teaching *all* our writers to be willing and able to write in a number and variety of genres, but especially our reluctant writers.

Action plans can take up a good chunk of our writing programs. They do not, however, take up every moment of our writing time. We provide our writers with open, unscheduled time to pursue action plan writing, private writing, or genres of their own choice; some students will use this time to serve as peer editors. We may also set time aside to write together as individuals or as a community to communicate any of our needs, interests, and concerns that may arise during the school year. We recognize that many genres will be learned informally through choice and circumstance, and formally through action plans throughout the year.

Our writers need a balance of time for private, personal writing and public, whole-group published writing. Beyond the initial stage of whole-group experiential language learning that kicks off any action plan, we try to ensure that the writers can dedicate time to the pursuit of personal, private writing during the open writing sessions.

Our challenge is to enable our students to participate in three- to six-week writing action plans. Each of these action plans is designed to encompass the positive attitudes typical of process writing *and* the explicit knowledge of model and form of writing that comes from the genre writing approach. Each action plan demands that we not be afraid to both directly teach our students *and* let them discover aspects of the writing process on their own. The goal is to balance these approaches to create an enabling learning environment for *all* our writers.

Genres for Writing Action Plans
Presented in recommended sequence with poetry reinforcing all of them
Description
Autobiography
Personal narrative
Expository text: Inquiry and exploration
Review
Fictional narrative

A Balance of Direct Teaching and Process Writing

We cultivate enabling classrooms through a complementary approach of strategic teaching in a process-oriented atmosphere. The key components of a writing action plan are outlined on the next page.

1. Eyewitness event(s): Whole-class experiential language learning
2. Eyewitness writers' notebooks: Recording experiences
3. Eyewitness Organizers: Framing and extending ideas in written form
4. Read-alouds: Reading of exemplary writing
5. Write-alouds: Writing in front of the students
6. Open writing sessions: Choice of writing activities—doing private, personal writing; writing, revising, and editing writing action topic; or editing the writing of others
7. Student-led exhibitions: Talking, sharing, and celebrating writing

Shift in Teaching Practice
Implementing writing action plans that take a complementary and systematic teaching approach will serve our reluctant writers well.

Based on more than 10 years of experience, I know that we can meet the needs of our most untalented, unresponsive reluctant writers, our most talented, responsive writers, and the prescribed curriculum through the use of action plans.

What a Full Writing Action Plan Looks Like

What follows is an outline of one writing action plan based on biography: "Life Styles of the Not So Rich but Famous."

Enter famous writer and poet extraordinaire: Robert Service! In guise as the poet, I am wearing a heavy parka to cover much of my face and head. I introduce the class to a biography writing action plan with our first event, a surprise visit by Robert Service to tell them about his life and read one of his famous poems, "The Cremation of Sam McGee." The students use their notebooks to record their free flow of noticings (first draft only, no mark given).

The next writing session I read a biography on Robert Service. It is my first read-aloud, taking up 20 minutes or so before I prompt students to pursue some personal choice writing in their notebooks.

The following session I write a free-verse biographical poem in front of the students as my first write-aloud, followed by some open writing. The students bring in examples of biographies off the Internet and out of books and magazines to read for our next few read-alouds. I model how I collect and organize information on a planning paper, an organizer focused on Robert Service—this, too, is a write-aloud.

After this cohesive introduction to biography, I finally invite the writers to choose a famous person as a biography subject. From a list of more than 100 people, the students discuss who would be good choices of biography. They record 5 to 10 choices in their notebooks as entry points into the writing action plan and then in the next couple of days seriously consider who to write about.

The next three to six sessions of the focused genre action plan begin with a read-aloud (to hear more biographies, such as ones on Terry Fox and Pierre Elliott Trudeau) or begin with a write-aloud (to see the biography), which further immerses the writers into the form and function of biographies. The remainder of each writing session is dedicated to organizing their ideas on biography organizers, which provide helpful prompts about information required. We shape big chunks of our open writing sessions around their constructing a strong biographical text and a free-verse bio-poem. Some students act as peer editors during these sessions.

Our "Life Styles of the Not So Rich, but Famous" writing action plan culminates with student-led exhibitions. Two or three students take about 20 minutes each to share their biographies and their experiences writing the biographies after a short, timed free write by the whole class. I now understand Steven's special request to shift his genre writing to an autobiography when he arrives in his hockey gear with his number "99" jersey tucked in at his side, to share his student-led exhibition! He proves to be more than star hockey player Wayne Gretzky—he is a star writer, as well (and a good actor too!). Every member of the writing community takes part.

How Writing Action Components Work

We introduce our reluctant writers to each new writing action plan by generating a formal title or name for it together. Here are a few examples:

Expository Genres
Goop, Glop, and Science Soup (Description)
Cool Questions for Curious Kids (Inquiry and Exploration)
The Quest for the Best Books (Review)

Narrative Genres
Now You Tell Me (Personal Narrative)
When I Was Young Scar Stories (Memoir)
The Lives, Times, and Words of Those Who Have
    Changed the World (Biography)
Me and My World (Autobiography)
Adventures of the Heart (Fictional Narrative)

Once we have clearly framed the learning with all our writers for a writing action plan, we nurture them through this complementary approach to writing with these components:

Introductory Eyewitness Events: We kick off each action plan with a splashy introductory Eyewitness event. As a class, we spend quality time together enjoying interesting activities where our writers learn to behave and express themselves as authentic authors. Eyewitness events are experiential learning sessions designed to get students discovering topics and a flow of ideas in prose and free-verse poetry. Our writers express themselves as authentic authors in special notebooks.

> I remember the first time I ever gave good quality writers' notebooks to my Grade 5s. Hugs. I got hugs. Not planned and expected hugs like you are required to give to great aunts at family gatherings, but the sudden desperate hugs of someone saying good bye for a long time kind of hugs, as some of the girls left for the day with their new, special coil-bound journals. Some turned back to smile as a reiteration of their appreciation. It was a remarkable moment for me as a teacher as they demonstrated their great regard for the gift of a private journal at school. What I did not know at this special moment was the far more special moments that would live in the powerful entries they would come to share with me in the near future.

Open Writing Sessions: Reluctant writers spend some time in the process-writing atmosphere of open writing sessions where the instruction is response centred

Expository text includes essays, speeches, lab reports, journals, articles, and directions, to name a few. It explains something by defining and describing, sequencing, categorizing, comparing and contrasting, presenting a problem and solution, or outlining cause and effect. Expository text uses facts and details, opinions, and examples to tell a story.

Narrative text includes elements such as theme, plot, conflict, resolution, character, and setting. It uses story to inform or persuade the reader. Narrative types include personal and fictional, as well as biographies and autobiographies.

and less directive. Our writers work on publishing their writing or on drafting in their Eyewitness writers' notebooks and Progress journals. They thereby honor their needs, as authentic writers, for purposeful writing that is public and published *or* private and personal.

> Thinking back made me sigh and shake my head. I remember when I shifted my teaching practice to leave the students to orient themselves in the open writing session. I remember thinking that I was ok with the first part of the writing session—the read-aloud, where I am the teacher and I am in control and I can make sure they learn something. What I wasn't so sure of was letting go for the second part of the session—just letting them go like that. It seemed so unnatural to just expect that they would make good use of their writing time; it didn't seem like it was really going to work, especially for the reluctant writers I had in this particular class!
>
> My giggle came one year later from the realization that the students are well able to sustain themselves as writers on days like today for the entire morning! I used to be worried about getting them to write for half an hour; now I worry that they will groan when I shut things down after three hours.
>
> Who says kids don't like to take control of their lives as writers?

Read-Alouds or Write-Alouds: Each session of the writing action plan is broken into two parts. For the first 20 to 30 minutes, there are formal teacher-directed read-alouds to expose our writers to the wonderful sound of exemplary writing followed by some open writing time. Sometimes, we have write-alouds instead of read-alouds. The write-alouds expose our writers to the teacher as writer, modelling the process of constructing text. The students watch how the writing process looks for published public writing with an Eyewitness Organizer or for personal, private writing in Eyewitness writers' notebooks or Progress journals. We follow our write-alouds with open writing time, as well.

> I remember thinking back to Frank Smith's words to young teachers: "You can't teach writing if you don't write and write in front of your students." He was so right. I can't believe the difference it makes to their writing and their willingness to write to have them see me, as their teacher, struggling as a writer in front of them. At first, I wasn't sure I would know what to do, but then I realized we all know enough about writing to be able to stand up and write in front of our students. You don't really need any special lesson plans, you just need the courage to write, to stand up, and live out your own writing process in front of them. It really helps if you talk to yourself about your writing, of course in front of them, too! Once you have risked doing it once, you are forever changed. You are changed when you know that you can make a serious impact on your reluctant writers.
>
> There is no other way. It works better than any other thing you do to get them to write.

Eyewitness Organizer Planning: Writers use their open writing sessions to organize their own writing to go public as real-world published writing. As prompted by the headings on usually teacher-devised Eyewitness Organizers (see the template at the end of Chapter 5 and Genre Lists in the Appendixes), they search for the specifics of their subject, record them on their organizers, and draft specific details into prose and related, or companion, poetry they will publish for student-led exhibitions.

> I remember seeing my son with bits of paper with key phrases spilled all over the kitchen table. He must have had about 30 little papers, some in order, some not, and some on the floor (probably some of the important ones). I remember thinking that having little bits of information on paper worked well as an organizing tool for my daughter; for my son Zachary, however, that approach was a disaster. I wonder how many other parents watched helplessly as their children struggled with collections of research facts on their kitchen tables late at night. I remember thinking there had to be a better, less painful way to do this for all concerned!

Peer Conferencing: Peers help writers make the final touches for their student-led exhibitions. They provide specific suggestions related to the ideas, organization, voice, word choice, or sentence fluency of the text. Peer editors also make specific suggestions about the conventions of print and presentation of the text so that the piece may be published and presented as part of a student-led exhibition. The key is to have students share the responsibility with one another to improve their writing one trait at a time.

> Do you want to know the best way to improve the writing of your students? Give the job to the nine and ten year-olds. They will get the revising and editing done for you like nobody's business!
>
> You assign some good writers the task of sitting at a special table, you remind them to be kind and caring, you give them scoring guides and special "Peer Editor" name-tags, and away they go. Don't forget to tell them that even though they are called "editors," they will not just be editing writing—improving conventions and presentation—they will also be talking to the author about revising ideas, organization, voice, sentence fluency, and word choice. These students will be super editors and ease your load as the teacher trying to get around to conference with 30 other students. The writers are ecstatic to have the job and never miss their times to gather up one of their six writers and check in with them. Yes, simply amazing.
>
> One particularly able nine-year-old editor makes it a point to provide me with steady feedback on what I should know about her particular writers. As a Grade 4 student, she knows more about her writers than the student teacher in our class on her final practicum.
>
> Simply amazing what happens when you give up on trying to run the whole writing class by yourself.

Free Writes: Late in a writing action plan, we replace the read-aloud or the write-aloud spot at the beginning of our writing sessions with free writing. Our students write at a steady pace without stopping or pausing to develop fluency. They use their Eyewitness writers' notebooks for their free writes.

> I remember thinking there were going to be some students who would have to struggle with our first few free writes. What was I going to do if they stopped and said they had nothing to write?
>
> Well, it happened. Devon was unable to write anything but his own name, over and over, which he did. After doing this a few times, he decided to switch

to writing about how he had nothing to write. He even volunteered to read this to the whole class at the end of the timed free write session. The interesting thing was, he did keep writing when I stayed steady, unwavering in my conviction that I believed he would be able to write for the designated time—I had to truly believe that he could this. Devon went on to write willingly most days and on the ones he got stuck, he just wrote down his thoughts on not having anything to write.

Even Devon, my most reluctant writer ever, eventually settled into the ritual to free-write willingly and well.

Progress Journals: For the first 20 to 30 minutes of some open writing sessions, writers write in their Progress journals. The students write about the progress they are making in specific areas of growth and development, such as running.

I remember thinking about what would be the best subject for a Progress journal and not being too sure of this. What would the students say? So I asked them. Out of the blue, one Grade 6 boy said that that was easy. Running. We need to keep PE Journals so we can keep track of our progress in sports.

It had never occurred to me to have PE journals even though I keep a running log myself. I was thinking more about Math or Reading journals for school; it never crossed my mind to have writers keep Running journals. I also wondered about what the non-runners would have to say about this. As it turned out everyone had lots to say: the slow ones complained bitterly, the fast ones religiously recorded their time, distance, pulse per lap, shoe design, dress code, best drink to restore their electrolytes, and so on, and the ones who hated running had even more to say than all the rest put together! Over time it was interesting to see who had improved enough to graduate from the "I hate to run group" to the "I can do it" group. All in all, the students were highly responsive writers in their Progress journals as runners—and I know exactly how everyone felt about running. Next year I am going to try Basketball Progress journals!

Student-Led Exhibitions: We end a writing action plan with several student presentations each day. Much like Author's Chair, the students have the privilege of sharing their writing with the class; however, student-led exhibitions are more comprehensive than Author's Chair in that the writers spend time leading the students through a series of prompts to explore the text together. Writers sign up to share the texts they have crafted from their Eyewitness Organizers. There is a rich collection of newly published texts for the students as teacher-leaders to share as the culminating activities of the writing action plan.

I will never forget Steven's student-led exhibition. Steven's autism prevented him from ever using a person's name or making eye contact with anyone but his mother and sister. Yet, after seeing students in the class share writing at their exhibitions, he requested to do his own as well. I suggested to the teaching assistant who worked each day with Steven to script what he would say, so that he could be supported in his quest to share his writing. As it turned out, Steven refused to use the script when he got up to lead his exhibition and although he did not make a lot of eye contact, he did miraculously refer to his peers by name. I was reduced to tears to observe this powerful moment when Steven broke through his autism and connected with his outside world. I also marvelled to see the reaction of 23 Third graders as they acknowledged their sheer joy for Steven's accomplishment: they caught themselves from clapping at the end of his presentation with due respect for his discomfort with loud noises and instead gave him a standing ovation.

All the activities of one writing action plan contribute to the understanding of one genre *except* the personal writing that takes place in the Eyewitness writers' notebooks and Progress journals. In an enabling environment, our reluctant writers systematically over-learn to write willingly and well, one genre at a time.

Something to Write About

I recommend implementing a series of 8 to 12 writing action plans a year to expose the students to various genres and thereby expand their knowledge of forms of representation across the curriculum.

We plan many wonderful out-of-desk experiences for our students to discover new writing topics and ideas. These include trips to witness changes in the weather and seasons—wonder walks, weather watches, four seasons festivals, daring digs, moving mud puddles, wiggle walks, and bog jogs. We can construct mealworm mazes and curate memento and family treasure museums. We can set up curio cabinets with our favorite junk from our toy boxes. We can organize stuffed animal pet parades to stroll the school. We can set up imagination markets, where we make art from collections of recycled materials, and mini science fairs. We can also have our own cooking demonstrations and displays of family heirlooms as a history fair. All of this can inspire our reluctant writers to write— and give them something to write about.

When we design writing action plans with a mediated approach of direct teaching in a process-oriented atmosphere, we create enabling environments to teach the essential traits of writing. We develop a good steady flow of both private and public learning activities within each writing action plan to help our students become authentic private and public writers. As writers gain confidence and experience, they may become interested in pursue writing topics of their own choice. We can give them the opportunities to seek out partners who have the same writing interests. Together, we can determine if they are willing to try a new genre outside of the action plan we are working in. We give our reluctant writers enough significant, strategic instruction from read-alouds and write-alouds to improve their planning and organization and enough open writing sessions to develop their fluency and sense of voice and word choice. At some time or another, we enable all our writers as leaders through their peer editing conferences and student-led exhibitions. If we are to reclaim reluctant writers, it is critical that we immerse them in such enabling environments.

Let us now leave our overarching challenge to reclaim them and look at specific challenges to enable them.

The next page can be used by teachers to think about various aspects of a writing action plan and consider how to implement one. The various elements are explained more fully in the chapters that follow.

Teacher's Action Plan Guide

Date: _____

Title of Writing Action Plan: _____

Participants in This Action Plan

❏ whole class ❏ small groups ❏ individuals
❏ partners ❏ snowball groups (student leaders)

Curricular or School Connections

❏ Science ❏ Social Studies ❏ Art ❏ Music ❏ Mathematics
❏ P.E./Health ❏ Reading ❏ Buddy Class
❏ Special Events/Celebrations ❏ Other _____

Planning Guide for Writers

Personal Writing: ❏ to learn ❏ to express opinion ❏ to express emotions
❏ to gain self-knowledge ❏ to inquire ❏ to predict ❏ to review
❏ to create imaginative places, characters, stories, poems ❏ to use the imagination

Public Writing: ❏ to share ideas ❏ to inform ❏ to report ❏ to entertain
❏ to show friendship ❏ to persuade ❏ to instruct

Audience

❏ peers ❏ other classes ❏ parents ❏ other schools

Genre

❏ description ❏ biography ❏ personal narrative ❏ fictional narrative
❏ review ❏ poetry

Topic

Universal: _____

Specific: Is there room for the students to have the power, voice, and choice to select their topics?
❏ yes ❏ no

© 2007 *Reclaiming Reluctant Writers* by Kellie Buis. Permission to copy for classroom use. Pembroke Publishers.

2: The Need for Fun, Experiential Writing

The June afternoon is balmy enough for us to need to escape the confines of the classroom and attempt to court a summer breeze. It seems the perfect choice to nestle the Grade 5 students under the trees adjacent to the school for their witnessing of something ordinary—or perhaps extraordinary. Either way, it will be of their choosing.

I stand back to watch the students using their loupes. Some are following bark-dwelling bugs. Others are looking under rocks and stumps for surprises. A lone bright orange bag garners Kevin's attention. I am intrigued by this boy's attention to an empty chip bag stranded in the tall grass. He examines the contents and settles into some poetry writing about his discovery!

Kevin is having fun with this great find. He incorporates some of the nutritional information from the bag into an ode. He is pleased with the poetry that flows from his choice of writing topic. His writing is clever and tells me about the subtle humor of this bright young writer.

The anxiety is gone! I recall when Kevin used to sit in a state of intense apprehension before he wrote anything. He characteristically approached his work in a state of nervousness and agitation. I think back to last September when he was entirely reluctant to write.

I am pleased to see that things have changed for this deeply sensitive and caring young man. I am delighted to finally see him relaxed and confident enough in his writing to play contentedly with his ideas and trust that he can write!

The world is full of magic things waiting patiently for our senses to grow sharper.
—John Keats

This chapter is about nurturing our reluctant writers' discovery and flow of ideas through fun, experiential Eyewitness events. Our challenge is to teach our students to live wide-awake lives, where they feel like eyewitnesses to exciting happenings. We teach them to notice things going on around them as sources of their writing topics. Taking this approach demands that we go on great adventures together and write about what we notice, provoking them to want to talk about what they see and share their results with others. It demands that together we go on wonderful, curious, amusing, and at the least, interesting, writing adventures, all to be recorded in easy free-flow descriptive prose and free-verse poetry. It demands that writers keep their writing private in Eyewitness writers' notebooks with no expectation to publish it.

First, let us review the myths and realities of nurturing the discovery and flow of ideas; doing so will lead us into a discussion of four critical success factors and significant teaching practices to reclaim our reluctant writers:

- the need for social, active writing
- the need to know how to be an Eyewitness writer
- the need for accessible genres
- the need for playfulness

I just go for a walk and come back with a poem in my pocket.
—Robert Service

Making Writing Social and Active

Myth: Writing is a silent, solitary activity.

Reality: Writing does not usually take place at a desk (except for a few highly experienced writers). Writers write as they walk, talk, read, daydream, or sleep. They compose their thoughts when they use their senses to notice ordinary or extraordinary things. Some writers carry notebooks just in case they discover a wonderful idea or an entire story worth savoring when busy doing things far, far from their desks.

Challenge: Engagement is reduced to its lowest level for reluctant writers when they have no hope of being social and active during the authoring cycle. How do we make their writing social and active?

Meeting the Need

This critical success factor is about organizing reluctant writers to have lots of out-of-desk experiences. Our challenge is to appeal to their sense of wonder. It is all about taking kids on adventures where they are eyewitnesses to events that are worth capturing in words. It demands that our reluctant writers take part in a good variety and number of communal events to develop their habit of mind to discover topics and a flow of ideas from which to willingly write well.

These out-of-desk adventures are reminiscent of the Language Experience Approach we may use as primary teachers to first invite emergent writers into the writing process. This approach typically holds the attention and interest of our most fledgling writers. It gives them a brief time in their early school careers where they write with enthusiasm and share their stories with pride.

We return to this approach to rekindle this same excitement to write: an excitement that diminishes for some writers as they move to disabling environments where teachers are pressured to fast-track their students to be proficient with conventional print and meet the learning outcomes of a continually evolving and demanding curriculum. We resist the temptation to move these students forward too quickly; instead, we take the time to return to the kinds of experiential learning that once served them well to prepare them to willingly write and feel a stronger sense of pride.

Bringing writing or learning to life often includes tucking our Eyewitness writers' notebooks in our pockets and venturing outside the school. Our students enjoy social, active events with an emphasis on experiential learning in a variety of outdoor settings. We take afternoons to go on wonder walks, do weather watches, stop and look at mini-beasts in the trees, build crystal gardens, mix up magic mud, float garbage-bag hot-air balloons off the school roof, and construct mazes for our mealworms to race in.

Students enjoy working cooperatively on these real-world adventures to notice, talk, and record some of the wonders around them. As often as we can, we schedule trips out into the big wide world and bring chunks of it back into our classrooms. Many of our most enjoyable Eyewitness events will be science-based inquiries that most students find interesting. We immerse our writers in experiential science explorations that appeal to their sense of curiosity.

In other writing actions, we create Eyewitness events in the classroom. We spend time curating memento or family treasure museums. Our stuffed animals

Shift in Teaching Practice
We need to plan and implement social, active Eyewitness events to promote writing.

stroll on grand pet parades. We build sculptures from recycled junk from the school and homes of our students. We have camping days and discover things that grow in the classroom. Such events bring social, active, experiential learning back into the lives of our writers—as perhaps they experienced before coming to school—and they can use their Eyewitness notebooks to capture their most memorable moments.

We integrate a vast amount of the Social Studies, Art, and Literacy curriculums into our Eyewitness events. Along with Science, Social Studies is a natural starting point for interesting events. Students have intriguing, knowledge-building experiences examining primary documents, going on historical tours or geography walks. Students learn about democracy in our local government chambers or investigate family history in the local museum. They interview parents or grandparents for "When I Was Young" memoirs and conduct reflective research on historical events that have most affected the lives of their family members and friends.

We continue our Language Experience Approach by inviting guests to share their lives with us. We live other people's lives when we recruit interesting guests, such as wrestlers, authors, illustrators, dancers, potters, and veterans, into the classroom, or take the students out to work with them in their workspaces. We live other peoples' lives by identifying with characters, settings, and their situations, problems, and resolutions in movies or in plays that we attend together. What better way is there to prepare writers to write than through real-life, connected talking and celebrating with guests and events such as these?

Most young writers enjoy these communal events for intense discovery, willingly taking responsibility for their own learning. They even become eager to retell, relate, and reflect on their experiences or wrestle with what they know, wonder, and learn from our shared moments together. We invite our writers to make entries about their noticings and to include topics, sketches, doodles, and wonderings for future reference. We record entry points to writing, listing possible topics to be narrowed down later. It is critical to the success of our reluctant writers that that they spend writing time out of their desks, the classroom, and the school. If we are to reclaim them, we must situate their writing within the interests of their lives and ensure that it is social and active.

How to Nurture Eyewitness Writers

Myth: There are two kinds of students: those who can write and those who can't. The writing process is mysteriously easy for some and particularly hard for others, notably reluctant writers.

Reality: Writing is not easy for anyone. Writing is difficult work; it demands concentration, effort, and a high tolerance for frustration. Reluctant writers are from a group of students with a heightened sensitivity to initiating the writing process. They have had negative or unrewarding experiences during the early stages of becoming writers and have acquired "writer's apprehension," which causes them to avoid the task of writing whenever possible. They think that exercises that never worked for them work for the good writers and that writers have the whole of what they want to say in their heads before beginning to write. They have no sense of how authentic writers truly go about their writing.

We don't want reluctant writers to believe that they are the only ones who find writing difficult. They need to learn that *all* authentic writers have the same struggles to discover their topic, narrow their focus, and search for specifics. They need to see that authentic writers work hard to plan what they want to write and they don't have the whole of what they want to say in their heads. All of these sensitivities and struggles make, rather than marginalize them as writers.

Challenge: Engagement is reduced to its lowest level for reluctant writers when they have no hope of feeling that writing is easy or possible for them and they don't understand how to go about it. How do we nurture our reluctant writers' understanding that much of the apprehension they feel is common to all writers, not just them? How do we redirect them to work at how to discover their topics and ideas, as authentic writers do?

Meeting the Need

This critical success factor is about reorienting our reluctant writers' belief that the writing process is mysteriously easy for others and particularly hard for them. Our challenge is to remind them that writers are not special; they are simply ordinary people who choose to write because they have something to say. This critical success factor is all about teaching reluctant writers how to discover topics and a flow of ideas. It demands that our reluctant writers see and believe that they, too, are able to discover topics they know and care about and take up the challenge to work with them.

We have two wonderful ways to redirect our reluctant writers to see and believe they are writers. These complementary activities serve to help bored, distracted, and defeated writers feel differently about themselves as writers:

- Eyewitness events: learning how to notice or discover topics
- Eyewitness writers' notebooks: learning what ideas to write about

We bring reluctant writers into the writing fold when we cultivate their reflective capacity during each introductory event of each writing action plan. Each Eyewitness event nurtures their membership in the writing community, focuses on interesting, fun experiences, and gets them writing freely through

- sharing ideas and being responsive to one another
- being socially and individually responsible
- being independent
- being active writers/learners
- associating writing with fun and enjoyment while in the company of others

We meet our first big challenge to nurture our reluctant writers' ability to discover topics and flow of ideas when we combine these fun Eyewitness events with free-flow descriptive prose and free-verse poetry. Whether writing prose or poetry, reluctant writers need practice in how to become mindful of what to write. We use the term *writer's eye* to nurture our students' ability to see the potential stories in the everyday living of their lives, that they have so many stories to tell, that their lives are full of possibilities. We work hard to increase their ability to live wide-awake lives and to notice things that others would pass by— and write them down.

Shift in Our Teaching Practice
Use of Eyewitness events and writers' notebooks helps students find something to write about.

Literacy is an activity, a way of thinking—not a set of skills. And it is a purposeful activity—people read, write, talk, and think about real ideas and information in order to ponder and extend what they know, to communicate with others, to present their points of view, and to understand and be understood.
—Judith A. Langer, *Language, Literacy, and Culture*, p. 4

CLASSROOM BANNERS

"Big ideas," such as these, can be treated as banners or added to students' notebooks as a way to develop their sense of what good writers do:

Good writers have a writer's eye.

Good writers carry notebooks.

Good writers write about what they notice, know, and care about.

One source of loupes is a U.S.-based company, The Private Eye.
Tel: (509) 365-3007
Fax: (509) 365-3777
Web site:
http://www.the-private-eye.com/ruef/

For our resistant writers, the writing process does not begin easily and simply with the teacher's assignment of a topic. They typically lack the ability or the work ethic to notice ideas that are significant and make something of them, especially if they have been provided with topics and ideas throughout their school lives. They need to experience concentration, effort, and a high tolerance for frustration, as authentic authors do, with these events. It is essential that we reorient them to work as long and as hard as authentic writers do if they are to be reclaimed.

Magic, pure magic! Exquisite moonscapes of soft blue, turquoise, and flour white crystals glitter before us. It is the second day of school and I am eager to see the students participate in their first Eyewitness event. The Grade 4s and 5s each planted their crystals by mixing up the chemicals and pouring them over colored sponges. Everyone is excited to discover the growth of the crystals. They have jewellers' loupes (cup-like magnifying glasses) to discover the crystals and new Eyewitness writers' notebooks in which to record their observations. I have invited them to share any favorite noticings with their group or go to the chalkboard and scribe them for the whole class.

I scan the room to encounter any interesting information about my new group of students. I am always curious to see who they are and what their talents and interests are. One particular student I wonder about …

Gavin appears to be in a state of flow—focused and fully absorbed in the doing, feeling, and thinking experience of noticing his crystal garden. His attention remains highly focused amid the social, active learning. Gavin eventually gets up from recording his noticings to go and stand with some other students to share his discoveries on the board. He chats and records his findings before he returns to his group.

I approach Gavin and ask him how it's going. He proceeds to share nearly a full page of ideas that he has collected and recorded by using his jeweller's loupe to examine the crystals. I ask Gavin if he likes writing.

"Oh, no," he complains. "I hate writing! I am going to be a scientist when I grow up."

I look forward to the challenge to develop Gavin as a writer. I look forward to many more Eyewitness events where I will challenge him and the others to discover who they are as writers and how their writing can come to matter to them!

Identifying Accessible Genres

Myth: Personal narrative, memoirs, and poetry can be a way to liberate our reluctant writers and help us get to know them.

Reality: Although it has long been accepted that writing classrooms with an emphasis on poetry, memoirs, and personal narrative can be liberating for students, it can be inhibiting for many as well. We do not ask reluctant writers, especially wounded ones, or those with family histories and stories that are painful to share, to reveal themselves through their writing too soon. It takes courage and compulsion to expose their vulnerability. Some writers may be too anxious with the amount of self-revelation that genres such as personal narrative, memoirs, and some poetry demand. When asked to write about what they know best, these writers may be concerned that they will have to write about whom they are, and for many different reasons—cultural, psychological, personal—they won't want to.

In order to find their voices, inhibited writers benefit from working with genres that allow them protective cover. They need to be inspired and to connect with accessible genres, such as descriptive prose and free-verse poetry, before they can be expected to work with some of the less accessible, more demanding ones, like personal memoir. As they feel more comfortable, they will reveal themselves and naturally expand their writing to include a wider range of genres; however, at the outset of a writing program, they need protection.

Challenge: Engagement is reduced to its lowest level for reluctant writers when they are forced to reveal themselves too soon. How do we ensure that all of our writers feel safe to write, especially our wounded ones? What genres are the most suitable to lure our vulnerable writers back into the writing process?

Meeting the Need

This critical success factor is about having our reluctant writers work in genres that do not demand personal revelation too early in the school year. Our challenge is to choose writing experiences that will support our writers' need to feel safe to write. Such genres as description and free-verse descriptive poetry are more suitable and accessible for their first writing experiences. We must respect our reluctant writers' need for a protective cover, for now.

The first writing we do focuses on descriptive writing and free-verse poetry. These are the most accessible genres for our at-risk students who won't likely withstand the demands of personal revelation and exploration. We engage our reluctant writers in playful Eyewitness events, inviting them to record their findings as free-flowing descriptive prose and free-verse poetry in their Eyewitness writers' notebooks. We get to know them and their backgrounds and better understand who they are as learners and human beings before we explore topics of self-revelation. These genres give our reluctant writers a sense of freedom to put down their ideas without feeling restricted by style, form, or the sounds of their words. It is critical to the success of our reluctant writers that they work within these accessible, safe genres at the beginning of our learning time together.

We immerse our writers in fun learning experiences as observers or eyewitnesses with jewellers' loupes cupped to their eyes. With the help of these tools, we make this strategic shift to activate our reluctant writers' desire to write.

Loupes, or simple, small magnification tools, engage our resistant writers in their first Eyewitness events. We also use magnifying glasses, the naked eye (and our five senses), microscopes, windows (cardboard with a square cut out of the middle as a view finder), or windowpanes (cardboard with four window panes cut out of it) as valuable tools to focus our writers' attention to discover things that may not otherwise be obvious. Our work with such tools invites all our writers to go on adventures to discover subjects worth examining. We use these tools to capture the attention of our reluctant writers and hold on to it long enough to develop their own habit of mind to discover how and what to write.

Shift in Teaching Practice

It's a good idea to begin the school year with descriptive and free-verse writing.

Shift in Teaching Practice

Provide loupes to sharpen the writers' senses to notice.

. . . students realize rehearsal [of writing] involves living wide-awake lives—seeing, hearing, noticing, wondering and gathering all of this in bureau drawers or notebooks or daybooks.

— Lucy Calkins, *The Art of Teaching Writing,* 2nd Edition, p. 31

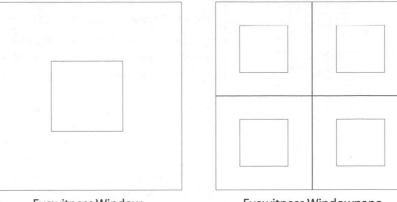

Eyewitness Window   Eyewitness Windowpane

Words About Wonder

Intelligence is not so much the capacity to learn as the capacity to wonder.
—Oliver Wendell Holmes

To be surprised, to wonder, is to begin to understand.
—Jose Ortega y Gasset

Wonder is the feeling of a philosopher, and philosophy begins in wonder.
—Plato

Good descriptive writing reinvents reality in the reader's mind with an intensity that rivals memory.
—Ruth Culham, *6 + 1 Traits of Writing*, p. 158

The big idea for the Eyewitness learning activities for writing is that as the students look through their lenses, the distractions of the world are left out. The magnification provides a sharply focused close-up image of a subject and makes the invisible parts visible. Our reluctant writers learn first-hand the habit of "eyewitnessing" the world: a critical success factor for them to discover for themselves, for their subjects, and for a flow of ideas for writing.

We use descriptive writing as a reliable starting point to encourage our reluctant writers to take risks. Wherever we are, we pen descriptions into our Eyewitness writers' notebooks with conversation as the medium for linking the two. We begin with

- simple attribute lists or webs (that may become the bones for pieces later on)
- writing and sketching of pictures with captions or diagrams with labels
- free-verse poetry
- easy traditional genres of poetry
- full-page prose descriptions of subjects embedded in genre studies across the curriculum

We follow three simple steps in the teaching of description with loupes and writers' notebooks.

Step 1: *I do*—The teacher models *noticing*, or the habit of mind to wonder by looking closely at something, with Eyewitness tools.
Step 2: *We do*—Students and teacher notice together, using Eyewitness tools (guided practice).
Step 3: *They do*—Students notice with Eyewitness tools (independent practice).

Observation, mixed with the prompts "What does it look like?" and "What does it remind you of?", engages students as eyewitnesses and leads them confidently into writing. Time to share their noticings and to record these in their writers' notebooks deepens and enriches their writing and learning.

The second part of the adventure with jewellers' loupes is to have the students ask these questions: What *else* does it remind you of? What *else* does it look like? This thinking by analogy or simile is an important tool of a poet or writer. Students can also theorize about their noticings by asking, "Why is it like that?" Intense, personal observations, as well as theorizing, help our writers develop more powerful habits of mind to continue their journey to become responsive writers.

How to Promote Eyewitness Descriptive Writing

- Let the students do their writing/learning activities in school time.
- Encourage the students to carry their Eyewitness notebooks.
- Keep the amount of writing they do open-ended—let them choose how much.
- Compliment those students who are willing to risk choosing difficult words.
- Refrain, at least temporarily, from attending to the mechanics of the writing; comments should reflect interest in the ideas and content.
- Encourage the students to share their notebooks with their families.
- Give the students a day or two to sleep on their ideas.
- Encourage the students to read the writing of other students.
- Encourage the students to read their writing to other students.
- Provide positive feedback, but no marks.

Returning to Playfulness

Play is a hallmark of intellectual life; playing with words and ideas is the essence of writing.

—Marilyn Chapman, *Weaving Webs of Meaning*, p. 62

Myth: A playful, fun Language Experience Approach to writing is too "primary" for reluctant writers.

Reality: Play does not just belong in preschool or Kindergarten; play is an important factor for the success of writers, especially reluctant ones. It is fundamental to a plan to refresh their enthusiasm for writing.

Challenge: How do we return to the kind of teaching and learning activities that supported the enthusiastic love of learning many students experienced in their early years in school? How do we best capitalize on the use of experiential learning—the same kind of learning many of them fondly remember—to reclaim them as writers?

Meeting the Need

This critical success factor is about initiating our writing action plans with playful language experiences, of hooking students into having fun noticing things. Our challenge is to design Eyewitness events that will contribute to our writers' enjoyment of writing. We explore some exciting, attention-grabbing materials or treasures, and traverse these with a free flow of descriptive writing or free-verse poetry. Writing about memorable experiences contributes significantly to our writers' enthusiasm to write willingly and well.

These Eyewitness events are similar to the natural language-learning experiences our students experienced before coming to school and in the early primary grades. We use these shared language experiences to cultivate the missed language learning of our students who are lagging developmentally, have learning disabilities, or have English as another language. For many, this is a "coming home" to the kind of learning that made Kindergarten and Grade 1 memorable to them. It is critical that we keep the need for the playful, personal discovery of ideas in mind when we plan activities for our reluctant writers.

Not only do we commit to Eyewitness events to teach our students how to discover topics and ideas, we also use them to get to know our students better

Shift in Teaching Practice

We focus on experiential writing, where writing grows out of experiences and adventures.

before we launch into the more formal genres of our writing action plans, such as personal narrative, memoirs, expository text, biographies, and autobiographies. As we listen to the conversations about what they know and care about, we come to identify our budding singers, scientists, historians, artists, veterinarians, chefs, craftspeople, and outdoors folk. As we explore wonders both in and out of the classroom, we come to know them as individuals and as a community. Real writing begins for reluctant writers with the playful communal discoveries we make with each new adventure we take—notebooks in hand.

Throughout the school year, we will continue to cultivate the Eyewitness habit of mind in all our writers. Reluctant writers typically need "eyewitnessing" experiences to discover their subjects at the beginning of each writing action plan. Playful experiential writing/learning is almost always a good place to start, to grab their attention.

Once our reluctant writers have had some great out-of-desk experiences and a few weeks of short, first-draft writing, all resulting in improved attitudes and fluency, we will begin to place new demands on them. We are ready to cultivate our students' skill to write in a wider range of genres across the curriculum. We will need to carefully monitor our writers' attitudes and abilities daily to know how to support and challenge them in the right proportions and at the right times.

When our Eyewitness events include writing that is playful, situated, social, and active, we are suddenly free of trying to push, pull, and cajole our most reluctant writers to write. We are also suddenly free to look to our next big challenge: to nurture their fluency through private, personal, and purposeful first-draft–only writing in their Eyewitness writers' notebooks and Progress logs. Let's take a look!

Eyewitness Learning

The two pages that follow can be used to help capture the interest, attention, and smiles of all your writers, especially your reluctant ones. Consider making an overhead transparency for each of the following types of Eyewitness events:

- Large-Group Eyewitness Event: Noticings
- Partner or Small-Group Eyewitness Event: Close, Closer, Closest

Large-Group Eyewitness Event: Noticings

Treasures, Mementos, Heirlooms, Art, Pictures or Photos, Specimens, Artifacts, Maps, Walks or Field Trips, Characters, Annoyances

Today we will write our "noticings" together.

Universal, general topic: _____

Identify your specific topic.

Writing entry point: Make a list of 5 to 10 subjects.

Select one: _____

- ❏ Select and look closely at it—narrow the focus.
- ❏ Draw what you notice.
- ❏ Write what you notice.
- ❏ Notice, draw, write:
    - ❏ What does it look like?

    (Everyone adds ideas to the list.)

    - ❏ What else does it look like?

    (Everyone adds ideas to the list.)

    - ❏ What does it remind you of?

    (Everyone adds ideas to the list.)

    - ❏ What else does it remind you of?

    (Everyone adds ideas to the list.)

© 2007 *Reclaiming Reluctant Writers* by Kellie Buis. Permission to copy for classroom use. Pembroke Publishers.

**Partner or Small-Group Eyewitness Event:
Close, Closer, Closest**

Universal, general topic: _____

Create a placemat poem: The group decides upon a subject or universal, general topic and records it in the middle of one paper. One student works on each of the four sides of the paper.

1. Discover your specific subject.

2. Look closely—narrow the focus.

3. Notice—Draw what you each notice on your side of the subject.

4. Write—Write down what you each notice.

5. Focus, notice, draw, write.

6. Read your descriptions one at a time.

7. Revise each of your descriptions.

8. Determine together the title of your text.

9. Present your text as a choral reading to the class.

Questions to prompt your noticings:
❏ What does it look like?

❏ What else does it look like?

❏ What else does it remind you of?

❏ Why is it like that?

© 2007 *Reclaiming Reluctant Writers* by Kellie Buis. Permission to copy for classroom use. Pembroke Publishers.

3: The Need for Personal Writing

I want the students to stand out on the windy field together, talking about how they feel, how their clothing fits, how their limbs, hearts, and throats respond to the chilly air, the sky, and the wetness of the ground beneath their feet. I challenge the class to be part of a concrete, lived-through experience for Running journal writing. I believe these students in Grades 5 and 6 will have strong emotions about their daily runs and that this kind of journaling provides a great opportunity for them to truly communicate about their first-hand experiences. It is my intention to ease one of my students, Kyle, into writing about something other than the mythical societies he seeks comfort in—and to do the same for other writers who are also stuck writing in one genre with only one, little, or no voice to call their own.

Bravo to Kyle! He goes on to write a number of well-crafted entries in his Running progress journal. He risks crossing an important threshold when he becomes responsive to writing in the present, of doing extraordinary writing within the ordinary act of going for a run. He proves to have a strong voice that clearly allows me to sense the person behind the words. I am pleased that he has been able to step outside of his preferred genre and be temporarily reclaimed as a responsive writer, willing and able to write with this specific role and audience in mind, and speak to me, the reader, in a responsive, honest way.

> When our students resist writing it's usually because writing has been as little more than a place to display their command of spelling, penmanship and grammar.
> —Lucy Calkins, *The Art of Teaching Writing*, 2nd Edition, p. 13

This chapter is about nurturing fluency in our reluctant writers. Our challenge is to improve the movement of their hands across the page and the flow of ideas with clarity. It demands that they get past the idiosyncrasies of being writers and settle into their writing. It demands that they have opportunities to write purposefully in at least two special notebooks throughout the year:

- Eyewitness writers' notebooks (which will include free writing)
- Progress journals

Personal writing remains the heart of the authoring experience for many reluctant writers. We do not resort to the teaching of isolated skills in these notebooks, but focus on the students' involvement in keeping track of personal writing topics with entry points of writing ideas for future writing and free writing. Notebooks serve a much different purpose here than the genre writing that we take public through publishing. Notebooks are strictly for private personal writing and not for publishing or formal evaluation. They are places for informal review by teacher and student alike.

We begin this specific challenge to reclaim reluctant writers with a review of the myths and realities of nurturing fluency to lead us into a discussion of five critical success factors to reclaim them:

- the need to keep private and personal
- the need to trust in intrinsic motivation
- the need to have choice in the task
- the need to recognize writing idiosyncrasies
- the need for intrinsic reasons to write

Safety in Private and Personal Writing

Myth: Writing in school is about recording information for the teacher. As seen by reluctant writers, it is the onerous task of fixing text through an uninteresting series of skills, such as spelling, punctuation, and conventions of print. Writing is little more than learning skills for skills' sake and serves no real purpose. Writing is boring.

Reality: Writing does not always have to be based on "fixed" assigned topics for the teacher. Writing can be deeply personal and done for the writer's sake alone. Reluctant writers need psychologically safe environments where they can express their ideas in writing without concern for adult standards of correctness. Some of them don't read much, have trouble with simple spelling and punctuation, and have limited vocabularies. Frequently, they worry about where to begin because they don't want to reveal their inadequacies with the printed word.

Positive, enabling climates do not emphasize correctness with writers in the early stages of their writing actions. If teachers push them too soon to revise their work, they won't be nearly as willing later. If teachers push them to evaluate before they have essential skills, they won't likely produce much and will have little to even work with. Patience is required. Learning to write involves taking risks and experimenting for all writers, but especially reluctant ones.

Challenge: Engagement is reduced to its lowest level for reluctant writers when they worry that they will be found out, that they will be forced to reveal how inadequate their writing is. How do we make our classrooms enabling environments for writers to take risks and reveal themselves and their struggles to us? How do we keep the writing personal and private?

Meeting the Need

This critical success factor is about having the writing our students do in their Eyewitness writers' notebooks and Progress journals remain as first-draft–only writes intended to cultivate this all-important safe writing atmosphere. We accept the writing of the students as they choose to organize it. Through our informal observations as they proceed to write without any prescriptive teaching of form and function, we learn lots about them. Our challenge is to patiently appeal to their natural language and curiosity to help them take risks in their writing. The private and personal writing that surfaces in their notebooks is critical to the development of positive attitudes and the courage necessary for the public published writing that lies ahead.

The important shift we make in our teaching practice is away from directive fragments of language learning to whole-class Eyewitness events: experiential writing events, where we activate the writers' curiosity and interest to write, and provide special notebooks to put this writing. We make a strategic shift in our

Shift in Teaching Practice
We provide notebooks for personal private writing as gifts so that our students can hold on to their ideas and look closely at them.

teaching to activate our reluctant writers' desire to write with gifts of bound or coil-ringed Eyewitness writers' notebooks. Students use their notebooks to make meaning of what they notice on their adventures. Writing things down allows reluctant writers to hold onto their ideas long enough to look more closely and carefully at them. Eyewitness writers' notebooks become invaluable tools to focus our writers' attention to record subjects worth examining, subjects that might otherwise go unnoticed.

Wherever we are—inside the classroom or outside—we collect all of our giving and getting of ideas in writers' notebooks. We share our ideas through noticing, talking, writing, and more noticing, talking, and writing about what we experience together. Reluctant writers get their flow of ideas by looking or listening to the rich and varied language of the group. We nurture a rich bank of vocabulary, phrases, and sentences that represents our collective ideas and understandings. The writers draw from the fertile collection of ideas and decide what is important enough to save as entry points to writing in their notebooks (see "Entry Points for Eyewitness Writers," page 42). We use these writers' notebooks to plant the seed that *everyone* is a writer and everyone has a story to tell.

We take great care in how we present the Eyewitness writers' notebooks to our writers. Some routines need to be organized for their storage, use, and assessment. We need to share our reverence for these books and model the kind of writing we expect students to do in them. We begin using notebooks with these considerations in mind:

Notebook Use Expectations

Students are expected to

• model reverence—deep respect
• put their names in their notebooks
• personalize their notebooks
• date all entries and keep all pages
• keep their notebooks safe
• carry their notebooks wherever they go
• take time to reread their notes
• rethink and rewrite
• draw on entries when meeting with others to talk, question, wonder, and compare

1. We take some time to talk about our expectations for the care and use of this notebook. We set up the guidelines with the students, making clear that no one reads a notebook without permission from the owner. On the one hand, we establish that we will not correct or mark the notebooks, insist that students put entries in their notebooks, or have students show any writing unless they are willing. On the other hand, students are expected to treat their notebooks with "reverence"—to hold them in deep respect. They need to put their names in their notebooks, keep them safe, and carry them wherever they go. They are also expected to date entries, keep all pages, take time to reread notes, rethink and rewrite, and use their notebooks as a basis to meet with others to talk, question, wonder, and compare. (See the summary of expectations in the margin.)

2. We hand the notebooks out a day before the students make their first entry, and let them decorate the notebooks with stickers, tabs, sketches, and pictures, personalizing them. We provide special covers for the notebooks to give them a special look or find wonderful coil-bound ones to ceremoniously present to the students.

3. We compose a list of expectations for the use of the notebooks, setting up the criteria as a class and posting them in the room.

4. We share a list of the entry points, or prompts, for Eyewitness writers (see page 42). These include favorite memories, trivia interests, and to-do lists. Students can go on to list possible things to write about and later short-list the possibilities.

5. We explore the possibilities for setting up favorite quotes and poetry lines, words and key phrases, and charts where students can describe words as delicious, tricky, personal, or textured.

Using Eyewitness Writers' Notebooks

- Prime writers with talk about the shared Eyewitness event before asking them to write in their notebooks.
- During write-alouds, provide demonstrations of how you will write in your notebook on the overhead; model the use of the space on the page.
- Remind writers to carry their notebooks wherever they go.
- Circulate while they are writing and talk to them while they are writing—don't clean the room or sit at your desk while they write.
- Give them more time than they are comfortable with; give them long enough blocks of time so they don't quit writing too soon.
- Encourage them to use their notebooks throughout the day at school or out of school.
- Have them settle into their writing, remembering that some of them need time for this.
- Invite them to share their entries with the class, making sure that they understand that this participation is voluntary.
- Respond to the thoughts or ideas in the notebooks, not to the mechanics of the writing.
- In a sincere and specific manner, praise the group on their efforts.

Trusting in Intrinsic Motivation

If the learner is doing the task to get a reward, it will be understood, on some level, that the task is inherently undesirable. Forget the use of rewards . . . Make school meaningful, relevant, and fun. Then you won't have to bribe students.

—Eric Jensen, *Brain-Based Learning and Teaching*, p. 242

Myth: Reluctant writers need to be motivated to write. The teacher's job is to prompt and cajole them to write and to give topics to write about, especially when they are stuck.

Reality: Teachers do not need to be cheerleaders. They do not need to assume that writing is a dreaded activity for which they must constantly push, lure, motivate, bribe, and reward students. It is not the teachers' job to motivate reluctant writers through prompting, cajoling, and setting out topics and ideas for them. Instead, they need to believe that students have deeply human reasons to write and establish conditions where students will discover these and decide for themselves how and what to write.

Teachers cannot truly revive reluctant writers with motivational techniques, discipline, or behavior management strategies. Attempts to control them from the outside have most likely already failed. When teachers try to motivate writers from the outside in, they send them, however unintentionally, strong messages that writing is an inherently undesirable task and that they, as teachers, need to go to great lengths to activate their desire to do it.

Cajoling may have a slight impact on some writers, but it is unlikely that it will entice the most reluctant ones into serious, authentic writing. Typically, reluctant writers will continue to "get by" doing as little as possible. They select to do just enough for the teacher or their parent(s), but certainly not enough to feel competent and satisfied as writers desirous of writing well.

In reality, most writers, even reluctant writers, do not have a shortage of ideas. Most of them have too many ideas and have not learned how to discover their subject or what ideas they should develop—this has always been done for them. It is critical that teachers revive reluctant writers' own instincts as authentic writers and not inadvertently give them the kind of prompting that suggests they are not capable of making these decisions on their own. Any deeply human, enduring need students may have to write can be presumed lost when teachers replace their intrinsic motivation with prompts, story starters, and "cajoled" topics.

Challenge: Engagement is reduced to its lowest level for reluctant writers when they are cajoled or told what to write. How do we activate their intrinsic needs and desires to write again without cajoling and controlling their writing?

Meeting the Need

This critical success factor is about enabling reluctant writers to take control of their writing with the use of entry points in their Eyewitness notebooks. Our challenge is to revive their instincts to be internally motivated by inviting them to shape their own designs for writing—not take ours. It is all about reviving them with the freedom, choice, and responsibility to record what they decide to know and care about. It demands that our reluctant writers discover their topics and flow of ideas from the inside out, not outside in. We don't force-feed them teacher-directed topics and ideas of what to write. Instead of prompting and cajoling to control their discovery and flow of ideas, we give them practical strategies, such as entry points, to help them discover topics and narrow these down to determine what to write from the inside out.

Entry points to discover writing ideas

For many resistant writers, this open-ended invitation to have choice of what to write can be as daunting as having no choice at all. Students need some strategies to discover what to write along with how to write. The big idea for establishing the use of writers' notebooks is for us to be able to more systematically monitor and adjust how they collect their noticings and discover subjects for longer pieces of writing. Writers sift up to 10 possible writing topics or subjects and choose one of these entry, or starting, points for their writing. Some writers may have several entry points and explore them until seeing which is most interesting.

We teach our reluctant writers to keep entry point lists in their notebooks and add to them as new interests arise. We remind them that they are not stuck with these topics; the topics are for future reference. We teach them to collect many entry points—many possible topics—and to record these in their Eyewitness writers' notebooks, clustered in groups of 5 to 10 and then winnowed down to 2. Key entry points include family stories, scar stories, interesting things that grow, birthday memories, favorite books, sports, hobbies, and interests, and home adventure stories.

- *Entry Points for Memoirs:* We can model how to make entry points for our memoirs about feeling uncomfortable (nervous, scared, excited, or sad). We ask the writers to list 5 to 10 possible incidents when they felt uncomfortable. We write our list in front of the students. It is important that we model our own passions, struggles, and risk taking as writers. We don't judge the students' choices, but work with them to afford them choice, power, and experience to narrow their field to which incident they are most willing and able to write about.

- *Entry Points for Reflective Research:* We use our writing to ask questions. We cannot underestimate the importance of problem finding and question asking. Students traditionally answer questions, not ask them. Envisioning a productive question is often more important than determining the solution to a set of questions. Reflective research can provide students with a forum for asking questions. Once students have learned how to use an organizer on reflective research, they can set their own questions and begin their own investigations. The students can identify their topic of interest and list 10 possible questions related to it. From here they can decide which questions they most want to address at this time.

Providing Choice

Myth: Teachers haven't got enough time to do it all. For reluctant writers, learning about how to write comes before writing itself.

Reality: Reluctant writers are motivated, spend more time on the task, and are more engaged in their learning when they have some writing time with choice and control over the content, process, and form. They need enough time to progress at their own rate through their writing process.

Challenge: Engagement is reduced to its lowest level for our reluctant writers when they cannot pursue some writing of their choice. How do we create a supportive structured environment where our reluctant writers can progress at their own rate within the regular classroom?

Meeting the Need

This critical success factor is about nurturing fluency with invitations to reluctant writers for choice in our open writing sessions. The writers complete their organizer poetry and prose writing to go public (the focus of the particular writing action plan). We give structure to the open writing sessions with this required genre writing. The organizer work is the backbone of the writing session for those who need it, the time when some reluctant writers take comfort in an assigned, teacher-directed writing task. Open writing sessions also provide some choice for writers to select topics that have not been taught. Some reluctant writers may take comfort in pursuing writing tasks that are not teacher directed. Our writers are enabled through these open writing sessions where they are invited to keep private or go public, and work alone or with a partner in their choice of learning activities. We take some time to orient the students to our choice-laden open writing sessions by presenting them with a range of options (see page 43 for a reproducible version).

An open writing session unfolds in the following way. At a set time, students have their writing equipment, including folder, notebooks, and pens or pencils, at hand. The teacher presents an introductory read-aloud or write-aloud, or invites students to take part in a free write (30 minutes). Then, a quick status of the class is taken—students are expected to know their writing plans (5 minutes). Students complete their required organizer writing of poetry and prose; alternatively, they choose to write in a genre outside of the whole-class writing action, for example, personal narrative or persuasive writing.

Session options for students include

- working on self-selected projects alone or with a partner
- writing in Progress journals, in which they retell, relate, and reflect on a certain subject
- doing free writes within their Eyewitness writers' notebooks, with one student timing and a set number of minutes for writing established
- planning new entry points of topics, ideas, noticings, and so on, in their Eyewitness writers' notebooks
- revising text
- conferencing with peers to improve writing through revising and editing
- meeting with the teacher for short writing conferences or mini-lessons
- working on computer(s)
- choosing what new learning to share with the class

In rare cases, reluctant writers will request writing topics outside of our required universal, general assignments. We take time to discuss their plans for self-directed learning with them. Their plea for independence may be a sign that we have engaged them as writers. Students seldom select topics this way unless they have a writing plan. We certainly want to differentiate the learning for any reluctant writers who request to step away from our communal writing topics. It is a sure bet that they will work harder on these topics than any other. We hope that this will be a rewarding enough writing experience to capture their hearts and souls as writers.

Recognizing Writing as Idiosyncratic

Myth: Entering the writing process and passing through its stages should be relatively the same for all young writers.

Reality: All writers have idiosyncrasies. Getting down to writing can be a very different experience for the members of our writing community, especially the reluctant ones. They have anxiety as they begin to write and pass through the stages of the writing process. Indeed, all writers probably need practice in putting their apprehension to rest and settling into the writing process. Some writers have already reflected on topics and have passion for their writing. Others have none. Some prefer to use pens, while others stand at the pencil sharpener sharpening new pencils. Some sit at an organized desk, while others spread out on the floor. Some have a writing plan; others have no plan. We create enabling environments when we recognize the idiosyncratic nature of writing and take it into consideration when planning writing activities.

Challenge: Engagement is reduced to its lowest level for reluctant writers when there is no hope for them to settle into their writing. How do we shift our teaching practice so that our writers are not ill served by time constraints and their immediate writing conditions? How do we acknowledge to our writers that writing behavior may very well be idiosyncratic?

Meeting the Need

This critical success factor is about creating enabling environments for reluctant writers to pass through their idiosyncratic moments into fluent writing. It demands we use free writes at the start of some writing sessions to reduce their apprehension, shifting them from a state of avoidance to relaxation. We plan to take their attention away from the anxiety about writing that prevents them from trying. We train them to do free writes within their Eyewitness writers' notebooks to turn off their reluctant writer voices, to loosen them up, and to reduce the vivid sense of limits they set for themselves. A routine of free writing trains them to get started and let their thoughts and ideas flow past their idiosyncratic stumbling blocks.

Our challenge is to get them to spill words across the pages without our critiquing, correcting, or rearranging them. The product is not important, although some writers may later develop something begun here during open writing sessions. Some reluctant writers make remarkable progress, and with routine free writes, become more fluent than they ever would have believed.

We replace the read-aloud or the write-aloud spot at the beginning of some of our writing sessions with free writing. Free writing is the process-oriented, non-stop flow of words across the page, most often done by the whole class. Our students write at a steady pace without stopping or pausing. We can free-write alongside them on a chart or overhead to model our own writing process or we can guide their practice as we walk around and see them write. Through beginning with a 5-minute write and working their way up to 30 minutes, many reluctant writers make leaps and bounds in their fluency. Our writers, however, need a careful introduction to the free write routine:

Free Write Routine

1. Review free write guidelines (see list at left).
2. Assign a student to set a timer (post time).
3. Ask some students to volunteer their topics.
4. Grab some chalk and head to the board; students grab their pens and have their books ready.
5. Timer says, "Go!" Everyone writes on any topic.
6. Timer says, "Stop!"
7. Have students notice things about your writing, words you misspelled, your less than perfect handwriting, your change in topics.
8. Point out that you didn't stop writing—you kept going.
9. Volunteer to read your writing to the class.
10. Invite students to share their free writing.

Over the course of many writing actions, be sure to vary the nature of free writes:

- Have informal nonstop writing in desks on any topic.
- Do informal nonstop free writes out in the world, in a park, or at the beach on any topic.
- Have formal nonstop writing events, where the whole class writes on a specific Eyewitness event experienced together.
- Let students do informal nonstop free writes on the computer.

Shift in Teaching Practice

Implementing free write sessions helps get writers past their stumbling blocks and promotes fluent writing.

Nulla dies sine linea. Never a day without a line.

—Pliny

Free Writing: Do's and Don'ts

Be sure to share these ideas with students. Consider posting a list on chart paper, whiteboard, or chalkboard.

Do

Relax.
Write, write, write—make it slow and steady.
Write whatever comes to mind.
Let your mind go.
Decide whether you want to share your writing.

Don't

Don't think—just write!
Don't plan ahead or criticize yourself.
Don't change or correct.
Don't think about spelling or punctuation.
Don't get distracted.
Don't stop.

Doing so will keep the free writes interesting for reluctant writers.

The class should spend several sessions producing first drafts until everyone becomes keener to write, and all members of the writing community know one another better. We, as teachers, have this time to "kid watch" and informally assess who our reluctant writers are. We learn lots by reading their free-written noticings and wonderings. First-draft-only writes contribute to our students' positive attitudes and fluency, especially for those feeling the gap widen between what they write and what others in their class or grade write.

> Everyone has to begin somewhere. I pulled a newly arrived Grade 4 student, Jacob, aside. Jacob, at three schools in four years, had successfully avoided the painstakingly difficult task of making scribbles on the page. I showed him how to handwrite two letters of the alphabet: *l* and *t*—printing had been such an abysmal failure for him, I decided not to try that.
>
> Each day we quietly took a few minutes to prepare what letters and short words he would practise during his free write. Just like all the other kids, he would pull out his writer's notebook to begin a free write. Instead of writing stories, though, he practised a few lines with my promise to help him figure things out little by little. Each day Jacob added a few new letter names, shapes, and sounds to his alphabetic collection. I praised him for making his letters easy to read and checked his letter shape and sound correspondence. The more he practised, the more confident and able he became.
>
> Jacob left Grade 4 with a new posture, sitting up straight, shoulders square. He had gained good control over his pencil and found a sense of place to learn what he needed to learn at his own rate in the company of his peers.

Arousing Real Reasons to Write

Myth: Writing is for the transmission of information.

Reality: Writing has many values to students beyond information processing. It has many functions in our society and in our personal and public lives. An important function can be to create worlds of experience for the writers, develop their thoughts, and thus have great personal value to them.

Challenge: Engagement is reduced to its lowest level for reluctant writers when they see no potential value in writing in their personal lives. How do we ensure that our reluctant writers discover that they do have time and choice to develop deeply human, personal reasons to write?

Meeting the Need

We give reluctant writers Progress journals to retell, relate, and reflect on the things they are doing in their lives and to give importance to them. When they are inspired and their writing activities satisfy their own needs, they put forth their best effort as authentic authors do. The reality is we create a brighter future for our writers when we motivate them from the inside out. Our reluctant writers have many ideas to write about, but they need reassurance that we are interested in helping them develop their ideas. When we know our reluctant writers well and have connected with them, we can begin to connect them to the

Shift in Teaching Practice
Use of Progress journals helps enable students to live wide-awake lives and to retell, relate, and reflect on their lives.

Progress Journal Prompts
Retell

I noticed . . .
I felt . . .
What surprised me . . .

Relate

This reminded me of . . .
It makes me think of . . .
I remember when I feel . . .
It is hard to believe . . .

Reflecting

I wonder why (how, if, when) . . .
Now I understand . . .
I now think that . . .
Now I want to know . .

Shift in Teaching Practice
Private dialogues within Progress journals show students that their lives are worth writing about.

page. We provide quiet, gentle support and encouragement as they find how to discover subjects in their personal lives or in our lives together.

Progress journals may be plain, school-supply sorts of notebooks, but they are not ordinary notebooks. We invite the whole group of writers to have a precious place to record the details, insights, and "goings on" of their lives. We provide special notebooks to capture the attention of our reluctant writers and to hold it; these Progress journals are places to reinforce the habit of mind to live wide-awake lives. Fluency improves when we activate students' motivation to write with a sense of purpose.

If we are attentive to current situations inside or outside the classroom, we can find some relevant topics that may be of interest to the group as a whole. We can draw on universal themes and topics to hold their writing attention to their concerns, questions, aspirations, or fears as tweens or teens. We want them to be free to retell, relate, and reflect on private, personal wonderings or public concerns and interests. These Progress journals invite the students to go on adventures to examine their lives inside or outside of school. They inspire our writers to look inward and outward at the same time.

- *Running Progress Journals:* Progress journals can be important records of our writers' improvements in some cross curricular connections we make. They can chronicle their progress as scientists, runners, writers, mathematicians, and more. Running journals are a good example of a rich theme for Progress journals. Physical activity can provide a wealth of ideas for journalling, given the senses and feelings they experience when running. Our students will all have stories to tell as runners. Good runners may rave about how they feel; poor runners may complain bitterly about being tired, injured, or miserable. Some will write about the heat, the cold, the rain, or the wind. Others will describe problems with shoes and shorts. They can each share their setbacks and victories. We use these Progress journals to further chronicle their past histories as runners, record their present struggles and triumphs, and outline future goals.

Progress journals can be dialogue journals, as well. We use these Progress journals to regularly exchange personal, private, or academic information and thereby let students know that the stuff of their lives is worth writing about. We set up double entry journals, where the writers record information on the left side of the page and the right side is reserved for teacher comments, questions, or reflections on the issue being discussed.

For some of our reluctant writers, keeping a notebook will be as natural as learning to speak; for others it will be worrisome, but worthwhile from our point of view.

We persist with the use of Progress journals with our resistant or "stuck" individuals, as Neufeld and Mate (2004) call them, so that we may form attachments with them and discover what matters to them. We want the reluctant writers to know that we are interested in their goals, passions, and aspirations. Honest responses can provide the basis for personal dialogue between us, a condition not present in the lives of many of them. We keep going with Progress journals in the belief that, as they learn to nurture thoughtfulness and take a reflective stance towards their lives, these students will be better off as writers.

We do not judge the Progress journals. We want the students to know that they have a place to record their musings free of a critical eye. We will however check that their work is there, that they are taking the time to reflect on actions. Here are some ideas to consider when using Progress journals:

1. Read and reply to each entry as soon as possible, and jot a personal note to the writer—doing this increases the possibility of dialogue and lets the student know you have read the entry

2. Never criticize or use a red pen. Journals are a form of expression and not a formal writing assignment (although it certainly informs your teaching for other times during your open writing).

3. The purpose of the journals it to encourage communication; they are not designed to be formal assessment tools.

4. Give the students an out, such as putting an *X* on the top of the page if they don't want you to read or respond to it.

5. Make sure they know that you must report on certain topics, such as abuse or suicide, if you read an entry that has a specific incident.

6. Don't force the students to stick to a certain topic should they meander away from the guidelines. The idea is to follow a set of guidelines, but also to allow for a free flow of written expression (your judgment will be required here).

7. Encourage trust as a key component to the successful use of journals.

8. Remember that some students will answer questions with as few words as possible.

The next two pages feature useful reproducible sheets that students can refer to when writing in their Eyewitness writers' notebooks or when thinking about how to spend their open writing session time.

With the implementation of Eyewitness notebooks, free writes, and Progress journals, we are suddenly free of trying to push, pull, and cajole our most reluctant writers to be fluent. We use notebooks to have our reluctant writers look inward to nurture an even greater flow of personal writing. When we teach reluctant writers to write strong texts that are fluent, we are also suddenly free to look to the next big challenge: how to enable them to nurture a sense of writing style expressed in such ways as word choice and voice.

Entry Points for Eyewitness Writers

- ❏ Subjects, topics, or things I am most interested in (what is important to me)
- ❏ Things I like to do
- ❏ Things I know about
- ❏ Things I wonder about (what questions I have)
- ❏ Favorite quotes
- ❏ Favorite lines from a poem (and why)
- ❏ Favorite people
- ❏ Favorite places
- ❏ Favorite memories
- ❏ Favorite treasure
- ❏ Favorite books, poetry, or movies
- ❏ Favorite pictures, doodles, and scribbles
- ❏ What good writers do
- ❏ Personal writing topics
- ❏ Family stories
- ❏ Scar stories
- ❏ Birthday memories
- ❏ Story outlines
- ❏ To-do lists
- ❏ Interesting things to make or explore (including "sciencing")
- ❏ Sports I am interested in
- ❏ Trivia interests
- ❏ World records
- ❏ Surprises I have had
- ❏ Noticings . . .

© 2007 *Reclaiming Reluctant Writers* by Kellie Buis. Permission to copy for classroom use. Pembroke Publishers.

Ways to Spend Open Writing Session Time

After you have heard a read-aloud, seen a write-aloud, or done a free write, you may be asked what your writing plans are and then given open writing session time. There are many ways in which you can use this time well. The ideas below provide a range of options to consider:

❑ Complete an organizer on a specific topic.

❑ Draft poetry based on organizer notes.

❑ Draft prose based on organizer notes.

❑ Work on an organizer project of your choice.

❑ Decide to work with someone and find a partner.

❑ Write in your Progress journal.

❑ Free-write in your Eyewitness writers' notebook—you will need a partner to time you.

❑ Plan in your Eyewitness writers' notebook.

❑ Meet with a peer about revising and editing.

❑ Have a writing conference with the teacher.

❑ Attend a mini-lesson with the teacher.

❑ Work on the computer.

❑ I help another writer.

❑ If you have writer's block, read.

© 2007 *Reclaiming Reluctant Writers* by Kellie Buis. Permission to copy for classroom use. Pembroke Publishers.

4: The Need for Imitation

Stories beget stories. Scar stories beget scar stories. Take Harry Potter for instance. The thin brand of a lightning bolt on his forehead tells the story of a powerful curse that failed. That, after all, is what Harry Potter is famous for. Harry, however, is not the only kid with a scar—and a good story to go with it.

I introduce the students to the idea of telling their scar stories through my reading aloud of my own scar story. Some scar stories are light and funny; others are heavy and sad. Teasing stories are some of the saddest stories we hear. Vanessa's story about her disfigured hand shocks the students who have been joking about it—some since Kindergarten. The students listen carefully, unusually silent and still, as she shares her story of the amputation of some of her fingers. This heart-wrenching story is a defining moment for the writing community where the teasing stops and the students truly listen to one another.

For a man to write well: there are required three necessities; to read the best authors, observe the best speakers and much exercise in his own style.

—Ben Jonson, *Discoveries Made upon Men and Matter*, 1635

This chapter is about nurturing the writing style of our reluctant writers through the direct teaching of exemplary genre writing that we read—and write—for the class. Our challenge is to help improve their competence in style through read-alouds or write-alouds at the beginning of many writing sessions. It demands that we also talk with our reluctant writers about the styles of good writers and our love of language.

We begin this challenge to reclaim reluctant writers with a review of the myths and realities of nurturing voice—the distinctive way in which writers express ideas with respect to form, content, purpose, and more—as they affect the following critical success factors:

- the need for immersion and repetition
- the need to hear the writing styles of others
- the need to see the writing styles of others
- the need for touchstone words, phrases, and sentences

Providing Immersion and Repetition

Donald Graves admits, "At one point, I realized I didn't teach; I just corrected."

Myth: Teachers spend enough time on the teaching of writing in their classrooms.

Reality: Reluctant writers need ample experience with purposeful writing in various genres to understand the abstract concepts associated with their design; they also need lots of background information through talk about these texts to gain the necessary insight to ease the difficult, foreign process of constructing their own. Teachers often think that genre is best acquired through students finding those situations where they really want to communicate something and writing for this purpose. Although this approach usually works for writers somewhat familiar with traditional school discourse genres, such as essays, it does not hold true for many reluctant writers. For many reluctant writers, learning school discourse genres does not hold any meaning—they have not seen or heard those under consideration. Typically, reluctant writers are not systematic enough, knowledgeable enough, or familiar enough with the texts of genres being taught to understand, acquire, or write in them. Teaching students with limited experience with genre through active writing for a purpose is not enough—we must do more.

Reluctant writers need time to write, preferably long sessions. Reluctant writers need immersion and repetition to *over*-learn the writing process if they are to write willingly and well.

Challenge: Engagement is reduced to its lowest level for reluctant writers when they have no hope of being immersed in deep and rich learning of how to write. How do we ensure that our reluctant writers have enough exposure to new learning not to fall victim to a superficial writing curriculum?

Meeting the Need

This critical success factor is about ensuring that our reluctant writers are not asked to produce writing in genres that they haven't first heard, viewed, experienced, or talked about. Our challenge, then, is to ensure that our reluctant writers know a particular genre so well that they will be able to communicate with clarity and precision in it.

We introduce our students to the abstract concept of genre through a routine schedule of read-alouds and write-alouds. To develop our writers' deepest and most abiding respect for good writing, we begin most writing sessions with read-alouds or write-alouds. Our students begin to conceptualize various genres by hearing and seeing exemplars of them. The first 30 minutes of each session serves as a ritual to remind our students that when we hear great writing, it is an invitation for us to be good writers, too.

Some days we do read-alouds, sharing texts that serve as strong exemplars of writing by well-known authors; some days we do write-alouds, using our own writing as exemplars. We use these read- or write-alouds to demonstrate the power and purpose of planning either to go public with our writing or to keep it in private notebooks. We want our students to follow our lead.

We select either read-alouds or write-alouds based on what best suits the needs of our reluctant writers. Students weak in the knowledge of how to write may profit from more demonstrations of write-alouds than read-alouds. Procedural knowledge of writing, or the explicit step-by-step process of how to write, is something that escapes our most reluctant writers who are thus hampered in their ability and desire to write. Students who are good procedurally, who are aware of how logical and sequential writers need to be, but who do not read a lot profit more from read-alouds. Some students will need a balance of both. At the end of a writing action plan, a student will have had many experiences learning the genre, learning about the genre, and learning through the genre with participation in read-alouds and write-alouds.

Repetition is a basic learning technique to use with our reluctant writers. Children use it to learn how to speak before they come to school and to perfect skills

Shift in Teaching Practice

We implement read-alouds or write-alouds at the beginning of our writing sessions—or keep and protect these important components of our literacy programs.

Shift in Teaching Practice

Repetition—and lots of it—is essential for reluctant writers.

in sports. Repetition is sometimes seen as boring or is dismissed as a tool to simply memorize rather than understand; however, for many reluctant writers repetition is essential. Knowing when huge amounts of repetition are needed is what often makes the difference between learning and forgetting and learning and remembering the essentials of good writing.

It is difficult for us to appreciate the massive amounts of repetition some of our writers need. Therefore, we often do not provide them with the opportunity or means to engage in activities that promote much repetition. Reaching the levels of repetition that will enable mastery of writing in a genre means that these writers need more time on task, something that many students who have trouble learning resist—learning is so difficult. Our reluctant writers need full authority over a genre before we ask them to draft writing in it and go public with it.

Over-Learning Genre Through Writing Actions

If we systematically teach a writing action plan for three to six weeks, we can make sure that our writers over-learn each essential aspect of process writing. We can immerse our reluctant writers in the over-learning of a genre in these ways:

- through experiential writing related to the style or genre—writing that flows out of an Eyewitness event
- through hearing and talking about how other writers write in the genre, using read-alouds
- through seeing and talking about the styles of other writers and how they use the genre—our write-alouds
- through approximating the use of the genre they have heard through read-alouds and seen through write-alouds, while working on Eyewitness Organizers
- through the sharing of 20 to 30 examples of writing style or genre use by other students in the class (see the discussion on student-led exhibitions in Chapter 7)

"I get it!" Beth cried as she jumped up, interrupting Jordy's student-led exhibition. "I get it—what a homonym is—it is a word, you know . . . a word that has a different meaning, but . . . but . . . yeah, it sounds the same. Yeah, that's what it is. I get it! Yeah, that's so cool!"

Almost every day for three months, the students had been sharing their writing at student-led exhibitions. Each author had asked the class to find a homonym as part of their brief talk about text and added it to the word wall which had swelled to more than 135 examples. Still, it took many experiences of hearing her peers talk about homonyms before Beth was able to fully develop her own concept of them.

Writing is learned by imitation. I learned to write mainly by reading writers who were doing the kind of writing I wanted to do.
—William Zinsser, *Writing to Learn*, p. 15

Hearing the Writing Styles of Others

Myth: Good readers are typically good writers. They can imitate the styles of writers by reading as writers.

Reality: Many good readers do become good writers through their own independent, silent reading of texts; however, many writers will also benefit greatly by being read aloud to.

Some writers become more aware of the nuances of the language through a read-aloud than they can when reading silently on their own. When exposed to the pacing and expression given to a read-aloud, they often hear more of these nuances of language, which helps them write better.

Those readers who become accustomed to skimming and scanning the text benefit from auditing read-alouds that move through the text in a slower, perhaps more methodical manner and consider expression as well as meaning. Although their comprehension may be good, these students may not have caught all the language patterns and nuances of the language that would help them with their writing. Many highly skilled readers skip words, phrases, and sections while reading and thereby decrease their exposure to a multitude of language patterns.

Much of what we know as writers comes from what we learn when we *listen* like a writer to read-alouds. Reluctant writers get their writing ideas from hearing well-known and loved books and by imitating the creative powers of talented professional authors. Many great writers emphatically claim that they acquired their own prose styles by imitating powerful, vivid selections from literature or nonfiction that they heard read or told aloud.

Challenge: Engagement is reduced to its lowest level for reluctant writers when they are forced to write without any sense of what good writing sounds like. How do we teach writers about the subtleties of writing, such as voice, which includes the aspects of unique author style, expression, mood, and sense of purpose? How do we give our students good read-aloud experiences to contribute to their knowledge of voice, the distinctive manner in which a writer expresses ideas?

Meeting the Need

This critical success factor is about read-alouds as an important way for our reluctant writers to hear exemplars of different language patterns that they may not by familiar with. Our challenge is to read aloud to them at a level above their own independent or recreational reading and writing levels—the levels they have mastery of—so we can expand their vocabularies and stretch their interest in and understanding of writing beyond what they can do through independent reading and writing.

Read-alouds give us plenty of exemplars of all the different parts of good writing. We can take time at the end of a read-aloud to record a wonderful example of a lead or a sentence or a word. We take a moment to record this example on the overhead projector, chalkboard, whiteboard, or on chart paper; we can also ask the students to record findings in their Eyewitness writers' notebooks as they listen. Students could work with a simple chart or headings, such as these:

Responding to a Read-Aloud Exemplar
Title: _____
Author: _____

Here is one example of something that I think is effectively written:

Features I noticed about this read-aloud:
I enjoyed the read-aloud: Yes or No
Why or why not?
It included what I wanted to know or was interested in: Yes or No
Explain:
It had features I liked: Yes or No
Example:
Ideas: It had ideas that appealed to me: Yes or No
Explain:
Organization: I liked the ending: Yes or No
Explain:

Style can be another word for voice if style is used in a way to refer to the characteristics of the text that reflect the author's distinctive way of speaking through the text; however, it can also mean the characteristics of the text, such as formal or informal. Style in this sense is related to the structure or form of the text.

Expression is part of voice where a particular manner of wording is used to convey attitudes or feelings.

Mood, or tone, is the emotional atmosphere produced by the author in the text.

Shift in Teaching Practice
We need to let students listen to texts as exemplars of good writing and to record some of those aspects.

A reproducible version of this sample chart appears as an appendix.

Organization: I liked the first line or lead:	Yes or No
Explain:	
Sentence fluency: It had words, phrases, or sentences I liked:	Yes or No
Example:	
Word choice: I heard words I liked:	Yes or No
Example:	
It sounded the way it should:	Yes or No
Explain:	

If we discover precisely what we like about a read-aloud text and determine what is good about it, we gain knowledge of how to become better writers.

Ideas: Is the writing original? Is there a good central idea?

We may enjoy, be interested in, or intrigued by the topic and ideas of a text. Sometimes, we enjoy a text because we are learning new things and the details are interesting or even "juicy." Ideas, such as becoming "real" in Marjorie Williams's *The Velveteen Rabbit*, receiving the first gift of Christmas in Chris Van Allsburg's *The Polar Express*, or having a mouse dentist clean the teeth of large animals as in William Steig's *Doctor De Soto*, are all exemplars of how authors have good ideas for their stories.

Organization: Is the writing organized? Does it have direction?

We may enjoy the text because we find it organized and easy to follow—we are not struggling to understand its beginning, middle, and end. It is clear. Organized texts with clear beginnings, middles, and ends, such as *The Wizard of Oz* by L. Frank Baum, *Peter Pan* by J. M. Barrie, and *The Lion, the Witch and the Wardrobe* by C. S. Lewis, all provide exemplary models to learn organization from.

We have excellent examples of organized texts with strong leads that hook the reader into the story. Among them:

"It was then that Constance did something that creatures would speak of in years to come." (Brian Jacques, *Redwall*)
"Now he is really going to eat me," Sophie thought. (Roald Dahl, *The BFG*)
"There is no Santa," my friend insisted, but I knew he was wrong. (Chris Van Allsburg, *The Polar Express*)

Sentence fluency: Is the writing rhythmic? Does it flow? Is there sentence variety?

We can listen more easily and enjoy a read-aloud due to the fluency of the sentences and the reader's *ease* in reading them. We enjoy hearing a good mix of sentence lengths and the rhythm or smoothness that they, as well as varied sentence beginnings, typically bring to a read-aloud. We listen to stories that have great fluency when we hear *Superfudge* by Judy Blume, *The Jungle Book* by Rudyard Kipling, and *The Sneeches* by Dr. Seuss. These authors provide us with exemplars of lyrical language that flows off the tongue.

Voice: Is the writing engaging? Can you hear the author's voice?

We can listen and enjoy read-alouds where the authors have put themselves into the writing, sharing their feelings and ideas, bringing the topic to us so well that we giggle or gasp, laugh or cry, engaging us and making us care about the text. Read-alouds that reflect a strong sense of voice are often the texts we enjoy and remember the most! Who could forget a read-aloud of Roald Dahl's *Charlie and the Chocolate Factory* or E. B. White's *Charlotte's Web*?

Word choice: Is the writing powerful? Do the words have color? Does word choice seem varied?

We can listen and enjoy a read-aloud with a careful selection of words. If the words paint pictures in our minds and convey clarity to the text we are hearing, we may really enjoy the text. Good read-alouds often contain words that sound the very best! Think of "frumious bandersnatch" from Lewis Carroll's "Jabberwocky," "fearful symmetry" from William Blake's "The Tyger," and "scrumdiddlyumptious" from Roald Dahl's *The BFG*.

In our read-alouds of exemplary texts, we likely take the mastery of conventions for granted. A key question to consider: Are matters of grammar, usage, and spelling sufficiently mastered and correct so as not to have attention called to them, but to aid the reader or listener in understanding the text?

Shift in Teaching Practice
We use read-alouds to train our students to recognize storylines.

Looking to well-known books can provide wonderful models of good language and writing to help our fledgling writers make significant progress. An appendix lists a variety of strong titles for read-alouds.

Read-alouds give us plenty of exemplars of writing that has great storylines. They give fine examples of the bare bones of the beginning, middle, and end of a story to train our students to listen for a story that is well constructed and complete. From time to time, we practise with a simple outline to teach our writers to hear a good storyline; by doing so, they are better able to develop their own:

Some Basic Story Bones

Story
Problem starts when
After that
Next
Then
Problem is solved when
Ending

Story
Situation
Rising action
Climax
Falling action
Conclusion

Story
Home
Adventure
Home

Story
The hero _____.
_____ stops the hero.
The hero wins (or loses) by
_____.

Shift in Teaching Practice
We strive to make writers aware of the sound and flow of sentences during read-alouds, to appreciate sentence fluency.

Read-alouds give us plenty of exemplars of writing that is graceful, rhythmic, and varied. They give fine examples of beautifully written texts that sound pleasing to the ear. We train our students to listen for sentences that are well constructed, to notice those that are varied in length and structure, to enjoy those that have an almost musical quality. When the sentences flow, we can ponder the melody they create. Read-alouds teach students to listen to the writing, to use their ears to hear what the writing sounds like. Too often, children look at writing and search for the correctness with their eyes. Read-alouds reinforce the need for writers to listen to an author's words—and to their own. At the end of the read-aloud, we stop and ponder traits of good writing heard; students may complete a scoring guide (see page 60 for a reproducible version):

Scoring Guide to Talk About Text: Read-Aloud

Text: _____ Author: _____
The higher the number the stronger the trait.

Ideas:	1	2	3	4	5
Organization:	1	2	3	4	5
Voice:	1	2	3	4	5
Word Choice:	1	2	3	4	5
Sentence Fluency:	1	2	3	4	5
Conventions:	1	2	3	4	5
Presentation:	1	2	3	4	5

Comments/Compliments:
_____
_____

Seeing the Writing Styles of Others

Myth: Teachers who do not enjoy and practise writing can nonetheless teach children how to write.

Reality: Reluctant writers need to see their teachers as enthusiastic writers. They need to see teachers as writers modeling their writing processes, their own writing styles. This modeling of struggles and successes with writing will be a more powerful influence on writers than anything else they may say or do to get them to write. Writers especially profit from explicit instruction in how authors develop writing in a particular genre. For example, when approaching the writing of inquiries or explorations, they need to consider the prompts who, what, where, when, why, and how. They will not discover many genres on their own—teachers must teach them.

Challenge: Engagement is reduced to its lowest level for reluctant writers when they are asked to do something that we as teachers do not do ourselves. Can we model the writing process of both public and personal writing, to activate the interest and engagement of our reluctant writers?

Meeting the Need

This critical success factor is about using write-alouds as our formal teacher-directed demonstrations of both public and personal writing. Our challenge is also to contribute this deep and rich understanding of genre well before we commit our students to writing in it. Our reluctant writers require careful, explicit explanations and examples of the genres in which we expect them to draft. We model how we take the information, think it, rethink it, record it, and reread it over and over. We use self-talk to make visible the invisible, or in-the-head, processes of nurturing this flow of ideas to collect, assemble, and draft our ideas into poetry and prose. Doing write-alouds demands we also give students explicit explanations and examples of how to draft writing entries for

- an Eyewitness Organizer (used for public writing in a particular genre; explained further in this chapter)
- an Eyewitness writers' notebook (used for private writing and free writing)
- a Progress journal (often on a specific theme; used for private writing)

Shift in Teaching Practice
We do write-alouds, showing how to draft graphic organizers called Eyewitness Organizers in preparation for writing in a specific genre.

In that way, students can see how and what they might want to write. We can also model the role of editors working with a piece of text to prepare our peer editors for their new jobs during open writing sessions.

We model how to organize ideas onto an organizer in front of the whole class. We help our reluctant writers when we reveal ourselves as writers following a carefully sequenced plan to assemble ideas into strong coherent text. To offset writing problems almost before they happen, we take time to ensure that the writers know how to work with any of the genres. We model everything from the first collection of a word to the creation of free-verse poetry to the arrangement of complete thoughts in a draft.

The amount of guided practice with organizers depends on students' needs. We can quickly model or use step-by-step guided practice to show how to construct text. In essence:

I do.
We do.
They do.

A partial organizer showing six headings with student notes beneath each appears below right. Note how the student has chosen to begin the biography with an appropriate poem excerpt.

1. *Filling in the organizer*

Students begin by making several decisions. They decide on their purpose in writing. They then determine audience, taking their purpose into consideration. They decide, too, on the structure or genre that best supports the expression of their ideas; then, they record specific topics to write on. They may make use of entry point lists of up to 10 ideas to help them narrow down their topics to one choice.

Once these decisions are made, it's time to collect specific facts on the topic. Students read, watch, talk, and notice, and then reduce information from their sources into key phrases of two to four words. They may determine how many spaces they need to fill to suit their writing needs, then fill in the empty spaces below each organizer heading with their key words and phrases, leaving the final square empty.

Next, students organize the facts. They color-code any facts that seem to belong together by placing a large matching colored ring around each; they then connect one ringed fact to another fact circled the same way. Facts that do not fit with any of the others are coded as well. These will stand alone and not be joined by a colored line to any other.

An organizer is completed when a student writes a topic sentence and a concluding sentence in the designated boxes, and also decides on a title and fills in the appropriate box.

Eyewitness Organizer

Who I know and care about

Purpose: _enjoyment/information_
Audience: _class_
Genre: _memoir_
Topic—Universal: _Biography_
Topic—Specific: _Robert Service_

Full name	child of ?	growing up
nationality	family background	childhood
birth, death	childhood stories	
Robert Service	eldest of ten	back to parents
English	grew up in Scotland	14 went to bank as clerk
born Lancashire England	lived at grandparents	published at 16
died in Brittany France 1958	got into fights—school bored at school	poems—paper

life as young adult	life	life
at 22 escaped bank	1896 to Canada	rough life
	rancher, farmer	poor
	lived on 25 cents	work in bank

> **Start with action:**
> There are strange things done in the midnight sun
> By the men who moil for gold;
> The Arctic Trails have their secret tales
> That would make your blood run cold;

Good Title: _Sourdough Songster_

Robert Service

Balladeer
Sourdough Songster
dreaming, roaming, writing
lingering in the northern landscape
on the trail of '98
Robert W. Service

Shift in Teaching Practice
We model writing notebook entries.

2. Constructing a free-verse companion poem based on key facts gathered

Using clean, possibly lined paper beside their organizers, students compose poems based on facts gathered. They create a first line with key phrases, put key phrases in a list, and play with the order of the lines. They then read their poems out loud and pay attention to the sound of the poems.

After listening to their poems, they revise and make changes to the poems so that they will sound better. They can add, delete, substitute, or move words around, checking first and last lines. Finally, the poems should be given titles.

3. Modeling how to draft specific details into coherent sentences and paragraphs

On clean, possibly lined paper, put beside the appropriate organizer, the writer creates a title. Next, being sure to double-space all writing, the writer creates a first line that generalizes what the squares are about, essentially a topic sentence, but without using details from the squares. From there, the writer combines key words to make a good sentence, combines facts in a sentence, or takes details and extends the sentence. As key words from the organizer are used, they are crossed out. The writer also experiments with use of a variety of nouns and pronouns to introduce the information, eventually constructs the concluding sentence, a restatement of the opening sentence, and reads the finished product aloud to see if it sounds right.

We can also structure a formal write-aloud, where we model how to record musings in Eyewitness writers' notebooks or Progress journals, displaying the value we put on the process of thinking as we write. As well, we can model our use of entry points and how we list up to 10 possible topics to choose from.

Entry Point from My Eyewitness Notebook

Topic: *Scar Story*
Possibilities:
1. *fall off skateboard*
2. *hit head on hearth*
3. *dog bite*
4. *broken arm*
5. *spider bite camping*
Selected topic: *broken arm*

Shift in Teaching Practice
We use our write-alouds to model revising and editing.

So far we have put our energy into nurturing a climate of trust with writing activities that do not require revision. It is necessary that we connect with our reluctant writers through first-draft writing before moving on to cultivating their better use of ideas, language, fluency, and voice. They will need our patience, support, and much teaching as they begin to develop the clarity and coherence of their writing through assessment.

We draw students' attention to revising as part of what writers do. Learning to revise their own work is a difficult, somewhat courageous task and one they will deal with only roughly in elementary school. Despite the fact that we are steadily moving our students towards products or conventionally correct text, that is still not a goal in itself. Correctness will be a significant part of writing as they get older, but we must not rush this—our rising numbers of reluctant writers is testimony to this impatience.

Procedure for Working with Organizers

EYEWITNESSING

Searching for your subject:

Make a list of 5 to 10 ideas and choose one. This is your *entry point*.
Examine the list of topics and select one. This is *narrowing* your topic.
Decide if this is the best idea to write on. This is your *topic*.

PRE-WRITING

Planning the purpose, audience, genre, and topic of your text:

Identify a real reason for writing this text. This is your *purpose*.
Decide who will read this. This is your *audience*.
Decide on the form your text will take. This is your *genre*.
Confirm the specific idea you have decided to write on. This is your *topic*.

DRAFTING TEXT

Collecting and organizing your ideas:

Slot in headings for the kinds of information you will collect. This is your *plan*.
Use this board to collect all your raw ideas and information for your writing plan. These are your *key points*.
Combine some of your ideas to make good sentences. These are *combined* sentences.
Group your sentences on the same *idea*. This is your paragraph.
Make a catchy, special, action-filled sentence. This is your *first line*.
Make new paragraphs for each group of ideas. This is your *organized draft*.
Give each paragraph a matching opening and closing line. This may help create a *strong* paragraph.
Doing this lets you develop your own writing—never plagiarize!

REVISING, REVISING, REVISING

Looking at your draft:

Revise your ideas. This is your *content*.
Revise your organization. This is your *form*.
Revise your sentences by reading smoothly out loud. This is *sentence fluency*.
Revise the words you have used. This is your *word choice*.
Wait a day to revise your writing again. *Revising is real writing!*
Leave your writing for a few days and read it out loud. *Writing is revising it again!*
All these revisions will give you your writer's voice.

EDITING

Preparing to present:

Give your reader a heading that promises what it is about. This is your *title*.
Check that your audience will be able to read the text easily. These are your *conventions*.
Check that your writing or the physical appearance of your text makes it easy to read. This is your *presentation*.
Now you are ready to take your writing public.

You have a text of your own making, with your own voice. You are a writer!
Congratulations!

© 2007 *Reclaiming Reluctant Writers* by Kellie Buis. Permission to copy for classroom use. Pembroke Publishers.

We will use our write-aloud time to model proper assessment of our own pieces of writing. We talk about our texts with the students to develop their ability to share the discourse of authors and editors working with a piece of writing. We follow a simple assessment scoring guide (see page 60 for a reproducible version of the one below) or use one of the excellent rubrics for the genre that school districts make readily available.

Scoring Guide to Talk About Text: Write-Aloud

Text: _____   Author: _____

The higher the number, the stronger the trait.

Ideas:	1	2	3	4	5
Organization:	1	2	3	4	5
Voice:	1	2	3	4	5
Word Choice:	1	2	3	4	5
Sentence Fluency:	1	2	3	4	5
Conventions:	1	2	3	4	5
Presentation:	1	2	3	4	5

Comments/Compliments:

_____

_____

We typically examine one aspect of the text, such as sentence fluency or voice, or we touch briefly on all major writing traits: ideas, organization, voice, word choice, sentence fluency, conventions, and presentation when the students have good knowledge of text traits. What is important is that we build in a time to talk about how to assess our writing so that we can revise and edit it to make it better and better. For now, we can model this process with our own writing:

1. Provide copies of your writing for the students to work with. You can either present a sample of your best writing or show writing that does not reflect the traits particularly well—students can respond to either.
2. Identify one trait of the scoring guide.
3. Ask the students to read the text with the trait in mind.
4. Ask the students to decide what mark they would give the writing for this.
5. Ask them why they gave the mark they did. You will find they soon get past any reserve about commenting on your writing and focus honestly on the trait.
6. Talk about how to positively address the writing, not the writer.

Touchstone Words, Phrases, and Sentences

Myth: Young writers cannot be expected to write with a sense of authority over the choice of words, phrases, or sentences. They cannot be expected to develop a love of the sound of language or to care about the language.

Reality: Read-alouds and write-alouds of poetry give students a window into authors' respect and power over language. When teachers pause in their reading at some words that appear to be "just right," they give the message to the students that words and phrases are carefully selected to connect with them as

---

Student writers, teachers, and peer editors *revise* for these traits:

ideas

organization

voice

sentence fluency

word choice

Pages 82 to 86 discuss approaching revision through questions.

Student writers, teachers, and peer editors *edit* for these traits:

conventions

presentation

So then, the one myth is that good readers will automatically become good writers. Not true. Many things about writing can be can be taught directly, but two timeless truths—the two most powerful ways to nurture competent writers—are to read to them, out loud, a lot, even when they could read it themselves, and to have them memorize great gobs of poetry, thus storing in their brain for life a glorious critical mass of reliably correct and appropriately sophisticated language patterns.

—Andrew Pedewa, *Classical Teacher*

readers. Authors and poets try to find just the right words; as authors, students too must take the time to be careful in their word choices.

Writers learn to be good writers by talking about good text. Talk about text is an important condition for uncovering what good writers do, what words they use. Teachers use read-alouds to talk about the use of great language and the writers who pen it. Sometimes, we talk about the text before we read, during our reading, or after our reading. Sometimes, we don't talk about it at all—we just read!

Read-alouds and write-alouds become social events where teachers immerse students in conversation about writers, writing experiences, ideas, organization, word choice, and sentence fluency, and develop their ability to think about language and develop a love of it. Taking part in a community to talk about text, including poetry, is important to nurturing responsive writers

Challenge: Engagement is reduced to its lowest level for reluctant writers when they see no modeling of the love of the language that enriches our lives. Can we nurture our reluctant writers' love of language?

Meeting the Need

This critical success factor is about providing reluctant writers with moments where we show our love of the language by the reading or writing of poetry. Our challenge is to take the time to ponder a special word, phrase, or line that may bring tears to our eyes. Our goal is to teach reluctant writers to recognize the beauty of our language. We must search for the specifics of wonderful language and make decisions to capture it on the page. Writers need to listen for favorite words, phrases, and sentences and make them touchstones for their own writing.

Wonderful Words: One Viewpoint

Great sounding words: meandering, mellifluous, murmuring, onomatopoeia, ishcabible, turbulent, Chattanooga choo choo, cuspidor, sycamore

Figures of speech: as pink as baby pigs (simile), the moon a ghostly galleon (metaphor), a smiling moon (personification)

Worst sounding words: cacophony, flatulent, gripe, plump, treachery

Ugly sounding words: fructify, kumquat, crepuscular

Words with lots of the same letters: tarantarratara—the sound of a drum; beeveedees—men's underwear

Special words: Mother

Theme words, such as those meaning scary: frightful

All writers have words that are personal favorites. Other words, on their own or within phrases and sentences, can be chosen to create great pictures in the reader's mind.

When we read from a great variety and number of genres, including poetry, we can draw students' attention to the use and misuse of words. We can stop and ponder the use of rich, colorful language: language that lets them see images so real that they feel they are in the story. We can stop and ponder language that is so striking, strong, and clear that it expands a description and makes something so real that students feel they are looking at the thing described. We can stop and ponder the power of everyday ordinary words, as well, to make stories sound

Think Aloud on Word Choice

"I wonder what good word I can use for the conditions of the sea as the frightened explorers headed around the Cape of Good Hope? I could use a word like *rough* or *wavy*. Now, when I hear the word *wavy* it almost sounds lyrical and happy. I don't think that contributes to the mood of our story. I want something more serious in tone. I think the word *turbulent* works better. It is stronger.

"The thing to do is to try reading the sentence out loud to see if it sounds right. Let's give it a go! … often through turbulent peaks and valleys. Yes, I believe it works."

Shift in Teaching Practice

We can combine poetry read-alouds and write-alouds to help revive the interest of reluctant writers.

natural and authentic. We can stop and ponder how words create meaning and satisfy the reader.

As writing teachers, we can read aloud poetry and recite well-loved poems to model our love of language. We can write in a variety of styles and lengths of poetry, starting with some short free-verse poems and graduating to longer, more dramatic ones. Poetry read-alouds and write-alouds can revive the interest of many of our most reluctant writers.

Our reluctant writers will not likely become poets through the strict, formal teaching of poetry models and literacy devices (e.g., assonance, rhyme, and meter) or by being left to discover it on their own. We can begin somewhere in the middle of these two extremes.

We strategically plan to have our reluctant writers become successful poets by inviting them to develop "companion" poetry for the writing in various genres they will do during the year. For example, they may compose free verse with their descriptive writing, bio-poems with their biographies, haiku with information text, or cinquain with personal narrative. (See pages 58 and 59.)

When invited to write poetry based on the same Eyewitness Organizers they construct for writing in other genres, reluctant writers can become successful poets. All our writers can greatly benefit from applying the work they have already done to develop the flow of ideas and words on their Eyewitness Organizers to poetry writing. Our writers also have another effective method to represent their thoughts and feelings. Many at-risk writers feel more successful writing poetry than prose. When we ask our students to represent their ideas through poetry, we know that they already have a good flow of ideas and can easily settle down to express their thoughts, feelings, experiences, and learning as poets.

We accomplish two important goals when we pair writing poetry with writing in another genre. First, by having the students revisit their organizers, we further deepen their new learning of vocabulary, grammar, and so on; second, we build their confidence as writers who can be successful. Using write-alouds to have students prepare companion poetry with writing in each new genre they learn is a highly effective step towards reclaiming our reluctant writers.

We help our reluctant writers by identifying a few appropriate poetry frames with each organizer. Each genre lends itself to certain poetry forms. For example, free-verse poetry fits well with descriptive writing, bio-poems go with biographies, and diamantes fit well with information text. The students can hang their ideas on one of the frames provided or free write poetry. It is important that they have numerous opportunities to choose what kinds of poetry to write. We want them to enjoy poetry and succeed at writing it. Many reluctant writers become confident, able writers through poetry in ways that they could not through prose.

With the implementation of read-alouds and write-alouds, we are suddenly free of trying to push, pull, and cajole our most reluctant writers to become more competent with some aspects of writing style. We use exemplary read-alouds and write-alouds to teach them about voice, including mood, and overall style, allowing them to hear and see the drafting of prose and poetry. When we model how to write and assess strong texts with voice and style, we are also suddenly free to look to the next big challenge: that of nurturing our reluctant writers' habit of mind to organize their writing.

Writing Companion Poetry from an Organizer

You can write poetry based on the ideas you have collected and organized.

- Use the organizer where you have already collected your raw ideas and data for your writing plan. These are your *key points*.
- Decide to free-write or follow a frame to write your poem. This is your *format*.
- Combine some of your ideas to make good lines. These are the bones of your poem.
- Group your lines on the same *idea*. This can be your verse.
- Make lines flow. This is your poetry *fluency*.
- Add, delete, invent, and substitute words. This is your *organized draft*.
- Give special attention to the opening and closing lines. This makes a strong poem!

Following this procedure will ensure that the writing is your own—never plagiarize!
Here are sample formats.

Simile poem: A five-line poem with a simile in each of the first three lines, three actions in the fourth line, and the subject revealed in the fifth line

Title:	*Winter Wonder*
Line 1: simile	soft as down
Line 2: simile	light as a feather
Line 3: simile	like thousands of tiny parachutes
Line 4: three actions	tumbling, gliding, cascading
Line 5: subject revealed	Snowflakes

Acrostic poem: A poem with a simple downward crossword puzzle; for every letter that goes down, a related phrase is put across.

B   Builder of incredible Lego
O   Offers to play on any team
B   Big heart, generous and kind to everyone

Bio-poem: Six lines about one person following this pattern

Line 1: nickname (created, if necessary)
Line 2: two describing words
Line 3: three action words
Line 4: four action words
Line 5: three describing words
Line 6: first and last names

ING poem: Topic with list that follows some pattern of verbs (action words), adverbs (words that describe the action), or alliteration (same initial sounds)
Animal Kingdom
Eagles screaming
Songbirds singing
Owls hooting
Spiders spinning
Cats meowing!

Cinquain: A five-line verse about one topic, as outlined below

Topic subject (2 syllables)	Treasure
Describe it (4 syllables)	special to me
What it does—three adjectives (6 syllables)	tarnished, shiny, fragile
How you feel about it (8 syllables)	my favorite as a baby
Another name for it (2 syllables)	first "spoon"

Senses poem: A four-line poem that follows the structure I see, I hear, I feel, I taste

Free-verse poem: A poem that is economical in choice of words with word placement not bound by form or the sound of the words

© 2007 *Reclaiming Reluctant Writers* by Kellie Buis. Permission to copy for classroom use. Pembroke Publishers.

Couplet: A poem in which every two lines rhyme at the end, for example:

To see an owl flying there
To see him swooping in the air.

Quatrain: A four-line verse that can rhyme any of the following ways: *aabb, abab, abcb, abba, or aaaa*

Sensory poem: A four-line poem that concentrates on the senses

Subject (name)	Rocket
Phrase (actions)	brilliant, flaming, flying
Phrase (sights, sounds, touch, taste)	a deafening boom across the sky
Subject (name)	space shuttle

Hello and goodbye poem: A theme-based poem with the words *hello* and *goodbye* on each line

Hello spring, goodbye winter,
Hello boots, goodbye skates,
Hello rain, goodbye snow,
Hello tulips, goodbye poinsettia,
Hello spring break, goodbye getting up early.

IS poem: A poem that uses *is* for the second word of each line; the same thing can be done with *are*.

Have you ever seen a …? poem: A poem where the first line is "Have you ever seen a . . . ? and the second line provides an answer with lots of *ed* and *ing* words

Have you ever seen an elephant?
Greyed, wrinkling, long eared, long tusked, stomping.

Shape poem: A poem whose words create the shape of the topic, for example, a star, a tree, a candy cane

Important poem: A poem that lists important things about a topic, with the last line including the word *most*

The important thing about hockey is that you are tough.
The important thing about hockey is that you play fair.
The important thing about hockey is that you listen to your coach.
The most important thing about hockey is that you really love to play it.

Haiku: A three-line poem, usually about nature

Line 1 (5 syllables)	snowflakes falling down
Line 2 (7 syllables)	in a whirl of dancing glee
Line 3 (5 syllables)	cold ballerinas

List poem: A rhymed or unrhymed list of things to do, events, observations, complaints, favourites, and so on

Three word poem: a poem with a noun, a verb, and an adjective listed vertically; the words should be on the same topic and begin with the same letter.

Snake
Slithering
Slimy

© 2007 *Reclaiming Reluctant Writers* by Kellie Buis. Permission to copy for classroom use. Pembroke Publishers.

Scoring Guide to Talk About Text: Read-Aloud

Text: _____ Author: _____

The higher the number, the stronger the trait.

Ideas:	1	2	3	4	5
Organization:	1	2	3	4	5
Voice:	1	2	3	4	5
Word Choice:	1	2	3	4	5
Sentence Fluency:	1	2	3	4	5
Conventions:	1	2	3	4	5
Presentation:	1	2	3	4	5

Comments/Compliments:

_____

_____

Scoring Guide to Talk About Text: Write-Aloud

Text: _____ Author: _____

The higher the number, the stronger the trait.

Ideas:	1	2	3	4	5
Organization:	1	2	3	4	5
Voice:	1	2	3	4	5
Word Choice:	1	2	3	4	5
Sentence Fluency:	1	2	3	4	5
Conventions:	1	2	3	4	5
Presentation:	1	2	3	4	5

Comments/Compliments:

_____

_____

© 2007 *Reclaiming Reluctant Writers* by Kellie Buis. Permission to copy for classroom use. Pembroke Publishers.

5: The Need for Planning When Going Public

It seemed to me that Stanley was one of those bright, capable kids who just did not do well without lots of choices in his learning. I wanted to give him as much room for this as possible in his writing. I paid close attention to our relationship and gave him a challenge to proceed independently with a choice of topic in our Know, Wonder, Learn writing action plan. My goal was to meet his needs by fostering motivation that would arise from the inside out. Stanley needed a truer form of motivation than what many reluctant writers get at school—he needed invitations to follow his own inclinations, not strictly my values and expectations.

I gave Stanley a organizer and a simple directive: to share an inquiry and exploration writing assignment that demonstrated excellent sentence fluency. He thought about this for a moment. He agreed to be the first student to exhibit a Know, Wonder, Learn nonfiction text. He also agreed that he would do this with words that sounded just right. Stanley didn't even bat an eyelash when I presented this challenge to him. Instead, he reminded me that he was an expert on sharks and that both his prose and poetry would sound great by the time he was done.

Stanley later captivated the attention of the students with his authoritative sharing of what he knew about sharks, what he wondered would happen to them in the next 50 years, and what we could do about the species that were endangered. He provided a great read-aloud of graceful, varied, and rhythmic writing of his research. Due to my support of his self-determination, Stanley had gone from being a student known for making some teachers' lives miserable to a valued and responsive member of the writing community.

Bereiter and Scardamalia (1991) have identified five areas of writing competence that are particularly difficult for the general school population: (a) generating content, (b) creating an organized structure for compositions, (c) formulating goals and higher level plans, (d) quickly and efficiently executing the mechanical aspects of writing, and (e) revising text and reformulating goals.

This chapter is about nurturing our reluctant writers' habit of mind to organize their writing. Our challenge is to teach them how to search for specific information and record it on Eyewitness Organizers. It is about teaching reluctant writers the procedural knowledge necessary to write in a particular genre willingly and well. It demands that we nurture our reluctant writers' confidence and competence in planning writing to share with an audience.

After reviewing myths and realities related to nurturing organization, we will discuss five factors critical to success in reclaiming reluctant writers:

- the need to search for specifics
- the need for choice in topic
- the need for revising
- the need for sentence combining and expansion
- the need for a flexible planning tool

If students are to make knowledge their own, they must struggle with the details, wrestle with the facts, and rework raw information and dimly understood concepts into language they can communicate to someone else. In short, if students are to learn, they must write.

—*Becoming a Nation of Readers*, p. 9

Given our efforts so far, we should now have clear signs of our reluctant writers becoming responsive enough to accept our next challenge: that of nurturing the organization of their writing for an audience. When we sense responsiveness in our reluctant writers, we make an important shift in our teaching practice from private, personal writing to published writing. We make this shift so our reluctant writers will pay attention to organizing content and choosing formats for their writing for others.

Making the Shift to Public Writing

Private, Personal Writing	Public, Published Writing
Eyewitness events	Eyewitness Organizers
private personal writing	public, published writing
Eyewitness writers' notebook writing for thinking and learning (self-directed)	Eyewitness Organizer work to publish writing for communication with others

Searching for Specifics

Myth: Once they have asked the teacher what to write about and how long the pieces should be, good writers plan pieces of writing in their heads. These pieces are written for the teacher.

Reality: Reluctant writers are subject to this myth. They are unaware of the decisions and steps required to generate ideas and assemble them for their teacher, let alone an audience. They have little or no knowledge that they need a plan of where they are going in their writing and should have an audience in mind. Reluctant writers do not know how to wrestle with facts or rework raw information. They have no idea of how to consolidate content. They have little knowledge of how to express ideas in various forms of representation for particular functions.

Resistant writers sometimes have attention difficulties, rarely communicating in writing because it takes too long to organize. They often jump around without a plan because their writing skills fall significantly behind their racing minds. These writers are more comfortable with talking than writing, and organizing their thoughts is a rather long and painful process. Reluctant writers, more than any others, need significant help to organize their writing.

Challenge: When our reluctant writers decide to take their writing public, they need to know more than the topic and length of their assignment. Engagement is reduced to its lowest level for reluctant writers when they will be graded on something they do not know how to even begin to organize. How do we equip reluctant writers with the procedural knowledge of drafting text willingly and well, and offset any setbacks (almost before they happen) that might diminish their growing confidence as writers?

Meeting the Need

Our challenge is to shift our teaching practice to help reluctant writers *over*-learn how to plan writing in the genre that a writing action plan is dedicated to. It

Shift in Teaching Practice
We may use Eyewitness Organizers
to systematically guide reluctant
writers through writing in a specific
genre for an audience.

demands that they do not jump into this writing without a clear plan of where it's going. It demands that they write with the reader in mind and search for the specifics that will best connect their writing to their audience. It is about helping reluctant writers use Eyewitness Organizers to search for and find those details that will make their writing come alive for the reader. Eyewitness Organizers are the compass points that orient reluctant writers towards polished, published writing: they give writers a strong sense of direction in the specifics of the content and format to write.

Without planning tools, such as Eyewitness Organizers, reluctant writers become overwhelmed, unable to find their way to effective drafting. In essence, we are holding them out of the drafting process until they are well equipped to draft confidently and competently. We can use these boards to cultivate rich collections of the specifics for their content and genre.

Eyewitness Organizers are tools to guide reluctant writers through the process of writing in genres for an audience. They allow writers to

- plan what they have to say—topic and subject (ideas)
- decide who they will say it to, that is, determine the audience (voice)
- work with the format (organization)
- research the specific supporting materials (ideas)
- commit their ideas to paper (sentence fluency and structure)
- dispense their words into poetry (companion) and prose (word choice)
- express ideas and thoughts as a writer in a style (voice)
- arrange these thoughts coherently in draft form for an audience (conventions of print and presentation)

Our reluctant writers have numerous decisions to make to take a subject and move it along until it is fully developed and unmistakably clear to the audience. We may give our students 11 by 17 inch copies of organizers with spaces for students to systematically lay out information: purpose; audience; genre; universal topic; specific topic; introductory sentence; specific details of content expressed as 16 to 32 key word phrases of 2 to 4 words each; what comes first, next, and last; what goes together; what should be added, deleted, or shifted; conclusion; and title—the last decision of an author.

Steps in process writing with Eyewitness Organizers

"We've rarely taught the craft of writing," writes Stephanie Harvey (1998, 53). Here, however, we use a carefully sequenced three-step action plan to help reluctant writers assemble their ideas into strong coherent text:

- searching for specifics and committing them to paper
- dispensing words into free-verse companion poetry (or from a choice of poetry frames)
- drafting specific details into coherent sentences and paragraphs

Students search for specifics by
filling in planning information,
collecting ideas, reducing these to
two to four key phrases, and
recording these details on their
organizers.

1. Searching for specifics

First, writers fill in the planning information at the top of the organizer: purpose, audience, genre, topic, and so on. They then read the headings or titles on their organizers and search for this specific information through noticing, reading, and viewing. For example, headings on a biography organizer would guide writers to find specific information on a person's place of birth, significant childhood events, family background, special abilities, and the like.

Eyewitness Organizer

Biography: Someone I Know and Care About

Purpose: _____
Audience: _____
Genre: Biography
Topic—Universal: **Human Stories**
Topic—Specific: _____

Students dispense words into free-verse poetry or follow a poetry frame by listing key phrases; reading them aloud to see if they sound good; adding, deleting, and substituting words; and giving their poems titles.

Students draft by color-coding key phrases that go together, combining phrases into sentences or extending phrases into sentences, constructing paragraphs from the sentences, and then rereading for fluency.

The headings on the organizer remind writers of the specific information they need to accumulate and assemble in order to write in a particular genre. When writers find this information, they deconstruct it into two to four word bullets (any more than this is plagiarizing), and record it under the headings on the organizer. The students pare down all their information into these short, key word phrases and enter them on the front and back of the organizer. The writers decide if they have enough information to continue with the topic as planned or if they need to revise it.

2. Companion poetry, please

Students create free-verse poetry or write in other forms of poetry from the sets of key phrases saturating their Eyewitness Organizers. Since this poetry will accompany the prose that students construct from the same organizers, it is known as companion poetry. The students select and order their key phrases into the bones of a poem. Doing this allows them to examine each for its relevance to the topic. They make decisions as to which ones need to be included, deleted, or shifted on their organizers for their upcoming drafts. In this way, the writers can finalize the ideas and data that best represent their subject.

3. Drafting coherent sentences and paragraphs

Once the collecting and sorting of key phrases is complete and the poetry penned, writers color-code the key phrases on their organizers that would best combine to make good sentences. They make their sentences and arrange these coherently in draft form on separate paper, crossing out each phrase on the organizers—some students like doing this best—as they use it. As they combine phrases into sentences, they "mix up" the beginnings, for example, also referring to raccoons as *these creatures*, *these mammals*, and *they*. They do this until they have a strong text entirely of their own making.

Eyewitness Organizers for Reluctant Writers

Eyewitness Organizers can be used across the Science, Social Studies, Health and Fitness, Fine Arts, Mathematics, and Computer Technology curriculums. Below is a sample list of ideas:

Description—Family Treasures or Heirlooms
Autobiography—Me and My World
Biography—Hall of Fame
Personal Narrative—Scar Stories Memoir
Inquiry/Exploration—The Three Rs
Review—Reader Response
Fictional Narrative—Home Is Best
Poetry—Bio-poems
The Appendixes provide outlines of headings that could be used on Eyewitness Organizers.

Enabling Choice of Topic

Myth: Teachers have curriculum to teach and topics to assign within this. They cannot let students choose what to write about and still meet their own needs of assigning topics required to cover the curriculum. Teachers need to assign topics so that writers experience all kinds of writing from impromptu journaling to formal essays.

Reality: There are times when teachers can let students make choices within the parameters of various units of study. They balance choice with and without parameters so that writers experience all kinds of writing, from self-directed to teacher assigned.

Teachers may assign universal topics: those general topics that are so deep and wide that everyone of every culture can relate to them. Universal topics are general by nature; specific topics, personal. The students select specific, personal topics under the umbrella of the general universal topic. Students use who they are and what they know to write these personal choice stories that will still be within the curriculum. The universal topics teachers assign lead to choice for our writers.

Challenge: Engagement is reduced to its lowest level for reluctant writers when they have no hope of writing on something they care about. Can we meet our curriculum demands of assigned topics *and* the needs of our students to keep their writing at its best? How do we teach all our students together and assign topics without creating a level of anxiety or indifference in some of our apathetic reluctant writers?

Meeting the Need

This critical success factor is about assigning universal topics to enable us to keep control of the curriculum, with corresponding student-selected topics, so the writers gain control of their writing. We have flexibility and control with the use of our organizers' universal and specific topics. Students can be spontaneous and pursue their interests, yet be part of an overall plan, part of a larger curriculum plan that has direction and purpose and a "big picture," or a destination to work towards. Students can be given a universal topic that fits well with the curriculum and within that, select specific topics. For example, a student with the universal topic of fears chooses the specific topic of encountering a poisonous snake as part of an integrated study of living things; by so doing, Science and reading and writing components of the Language Arts curriculum may be covered. Our challenge is not to be afraid to teach our students and have them all work on assigned topics. It demands that we make good decisions about the topics we assign.

Shift in Teaching Practice
We work with universal, or archetypal, topics that allow all students entry into specific topics.

In each writing action plan, we purposely work with an archetypal, or universal, topic that runs so deep and wide that every student in our class can relate to it. For example, we begin our memoir action plan with scar stories. What writer doesn't have a scar story? Our memories may be happy, sad, or funny, but we all have childhood memories of scars. They may be steeped in reality or dreamed in fantasy. No race, culture, gender, or religion is left out. Much of our best literature has a universal quality that everyone can relate to. The Harry Potter books, for example, provide a famous example of a character with a scar story.

Although the universal topic is assigned, our writers have the choice, voice, and power to determine their specific writing topics. Each organizer has a place for the writer to record the universal topic which may be assigned by the teacher and the personal choice topic that corresponds to it.

The best part of this use of universal and specific topics is the knowledge that students who crave choices have them and those who feel anxious, insecure, or fearful do not have to have them. When we assign universal topics, we are not taking away any of our writers' power or robbing them of their sense of ownership. We can be directive and developmental—and give them ownership all at the same time. We can implement each writing action plan knowing that we can meet the needs of writers who crave choice and the needs of those who do not.

Choice Within Universal Topics

Universal Topic	Specific Topic
scars	falling off bike
fears	chased by a snake
love	first date
memories	When I was young . . .
fathers	going fishing
grandmothers	gardening

Shifting and Shaping Writing

Myth: Good writers work with a systematic, neat, linear, left-to-right process that is right the first time.

Reality: Writing is less of a systematic, neat, left-to-right process and more of a shifting and shaping process. Reluctant writers need non-linear ways to lay out what they have to say, who they say it to, and what specific supporting material they need to make the writing ring true to the audience. They need open spaces to shuffle their sequences of words and phrases around. They need room to maneuver new ideas. They must understand that authentic writers also experiment and play with their writing to get it right.

Challenge: Engagement is reduced to its lowest level for reluctant writers when they are expected to get it right, when there is no hope for them to physically shift and shape their writing to organize it. How do we provide opportunities for students to discover the need for revisions as they go along?

Meeting the Need

This critical success factor is about providing reluctant writers with organizers that have non-linear, open spaces so that they can more easily add, delete, and shift their key phrases around. Our challenge is to remind them that authors do not organize in their heads; they organize and reorganize on paper or on screen. Our challenge is to teach our students to discover that writing needs to be shifted and shaped, wrestled with and manipulated until it has a form that satisfies them enough to want to share with others. It demands that our reluctant writers make many decisions about the selection and placement of the specifics of their topics.

Shift in Teaching Practice
We introduce the use of organizers as a way for students to shift and shape what they have to say.

It demands that writers learn to work hard to play with the order and choice of words, phrases, and sentences for their texts.

We meet the big challenge to nurture our reluctant writers' ability to organize their writing when they use organizers as places to shift and shape what they have to say, including the specific supporting material that will make their texts strong.

Organizers are formatted in such a way that there are open spaces to collect ideas. Ideas can be organized in several places on paper. Students create outlines without organizing them in linear, left-to-right processes. Students can move words around on the page; they can shuffle their ideas in the open spaces, keeping control of them. Ideas are not on little bits of paper flying around or falling haphazardly on the floor.

Constructing Sentences of Their Own

Myth: Elementary school children are too young to be expected to demonstrate voice in their writing. It is not developmentally appropriate for us to teach the writing trait of voice—this level of expectation belongs in high school with more mature writers.

Reality: Sentence construction through combining and extending is one of the most valuable writing skills reluctant writers learn in their elementary school careers. Students become empowered, responsive writers when they hear text that is their own, that carries their voice, mood, and style, not lapsing into plagiarized words from a book or from the Internet site where they gathered information.

Challenge: Engagement is reduced to its lowest level when reluctant writers recycle the words of others as their own and don't develop their own voice, mood, and style as writers. How do we ensure that we hold to expectations that our students will write with their own voice, mood, and style?

Meeting the Need

This critical success factor is about teaching our reluctant writers how to combine and extend sentences from the specific details collected on their organizers. Our challenge is to give our writers many opportunities to organize specific details into big bold sentences. It demands that our reluctant writers have opportunities to hear their sentences rather than look at them.

Shift in Teaching Practice
We teach students how to combine sentences for effect—and listen to what they sound like.

Reluctant writers need plenty of practice to enhance what their sentences mean. They improve their ability to make a variety of interesting combined sentences, of varied length, style, or structure with each organizer they construct. All these students begin to nurture their own voice, mood, and style by listening to, not just looking at their text.

Sample sentence combining activity, based on organizer data:

Robert Service	eldest of ten	back to parents
English	grew up in Scotland	14 went to bank
born Lancashire England	lived at grandparents	as clerk

These specific facts become a sentence:

> Robert Service, the eldest of ten children, was born to Scottish parents in Lancashire, England.

We take some time to teach our reluctant writers to take their sentence expansions and read them out loud to hear how fluent they are. They listen for the flow of their words to hear if they sound right. We specifically teach them to *listen* for fluency rather than look for it. We want all our writers to be thoughtful about the sound of their writing.

Students are expected to construct many texts in their lives. The organizers are not as important as the procedural knowledge students will gain about how to develop their own voice, mood, and style. It is our hope that rich process-writing skills, such as sentence combining and extending, will give them their own voice and style, and make them less likely to plagiarize books or Internet sources. We want to stress the importance of students using their own thoughts and ideas in their writing, an important ethical issue for all writers to address, but especially reluctant ones!

Keeping Planning Tools Flexible

As George Hillocks writes, the prescriptive use of models, imitation of patterns, and reliance on rules are ineffective for the cultivation of good writing.

Myth: Teachers need to use prescriptive models with their reluctant writers to assist them with the writing process. Nothing else has worked for them.

Reality: Teachers must be careful when they have reluctant writers use prescriptive models of writing. While frameworks can be helpful, teachers may overuse them. Students can come to rely on the pattern and find it hard to write without one. The writing can also become stilted and monotonous if the frame is not used correctly. The danger of standard frameworks is that students use only the template, improving their organization in the short term, but never moving beyond the recognizable pattern to generalize their new skills for independent use.

Challenge: Engagement is reduced to its lowest level for reluctant writers when they have no hope of having choice in how they organize their writing for publishing. How do we create a useful tool to help our reluctant writers organize their writing, but not have it too rigid and prescriptive? How do we get reluctant writers to move beyond the recognizable patterns of the organizers and generalize their new writing skills for independent use?

Meeting the Need

This critical success factor is about providing a flexible tool to assist our reluctant writers in organizing their writing while allowing for choice in how they organize

Shift in Teaching Practice
We provide students with flexible
frameworks for organizing their
writing.

their information—the tool should not be too prescriptive and interfere with their writing process. Our reluctant writers must have opportunities to use the organizers in different ways to differentiate their learning.

Organizers are designed to be flexible enough to suit writers of different ages (Grades 3 to 9 and beyond) and stages of development, to develop texts of various lengths and difficulty on general or specific topics, and to be used individually or with a whole class.

We provide varying degrees of teaching support for our reluctant writers. For the introduction of each new organizer of each writing action plan, we provide maximum support to the whole class. As the students become familiar with a particular genre, we need to provide only moderate support and reserve guided practice for smaller groups of struggling writers. When students have a strong background in some genres, they may not need instruction in the formal features associated with them.

Reluctant writers will typically benefit from more instruction in those genres they are unfamiliar with. Some low progress and at-risk students with limited spoken English may need continued support from teaching assistants, student tutors, and parent helpers with writing genres that are unfamiliar to them.

We help ELL (English Language Learner) students make connections between their first and second languages as part of organizer writing activities. Learning English should not diminish a child's first language: English is an additional language rather than a replacement language. ELL students may produce some organizers in their first language. Likewise, collaboration and cooperative learning are important ways of supporting ELL learners as they assemble their organizers in English. They will quickly come to know something about language and literacy by working with partners who are more able in English than they are. Our reluctant ELL writers acquire communication skills when interacting with peers in standard English.

Many of our writers are capable learners who prefer to be free of direct instruction; they do well with the challenge to have a voice and the choice to work on an independent writing project. Minimal support, perhaps some brief encouragement and feedback, is required for them to use the boards independently. We invite them to think, talk, and generate ideas on organizers that they have never seen before.

We may introduce the use of snowball groups, where we invite independent, capable users of organizers to become leaders and oversee small groups. For these leaders, we draw on our reluctant, yet capable writers more than our keen and capable writers who may not need or want this incentive. Our transformation of reluctant, yet capable writers into responsive leaders enhances the enabling atmosphere of our classroom. Learning to lead is exciting and challenging. It draws students into the writing process and into the community of writers, promoting success for many of our capable, yet reluctant writers.

Making Adaptations for the Use of Eyewitness Organizers: We can support and challenge writers who write little in the right proportions and at the right times by adapting their use of the organizer. For example, we can help reluctant writers who have trouble getting the words down by scribing what they tell us.

How to Adapt Organizer Use to Help Reluctant Writers

Consider making any of the following adaptations, which are based on how well reluctant writers meet the performance standard.

For Students Minimally Meeting the Performance Standard
- Give students a teacher-made, filled-in organizer.
- Give students a color-coded, teacher-made organizer.
- Give partners who are slightly more able to students.
- Give partners to ELL students.
- Scribe for the students.

For Students Fully Meeting the Performance Standard
- Give students a book at their level to collect ideas from.
- Create with the students a mind map of information from which to collect their key phrases.
- Give them partners of equal or different ability to work with.
- Give students two different sources to gather information from.

For Students Exceeding the Performance Standard
- Give students the option to find their own information through interviews and so on.
- Give them capable writers as partners.
- Give students the option to choose their own topics, sources, and partners.
- Give students the option to design their own organizers.
- Give student artists the option to draw their organizers.
- Give ELL students the option to work in their first language.
- Give learning disabled students, or those with large gaps between ability and written output, the option to construct their organizers on a computer.
- Give students the option to create organizers for the class.

"Know Where You Are Headed," the reproducible page that follows, provides students with reminders on how to approach their work on organizers—and how to approach the planning of writing in general. The next two pages provide a template for organizer development; suggested prompts for writing in various forms appear as an appendix.

With the implementation of Eyewitness Organizers, we are suddenly free of trying to push, pull, and cajole our most reluctant writers to plan. When we teach them to write strong texts through organizer planning to cultivate the strong organization of genres and companion poetry, we are also free to look to the next big challenge: that of nurturing the ability of our reluctant writers to assess writing for editing and publishing.

Know Where You Are Headed

Especially when you are planning to take your writing public, it is necessary to plan, research, rethink, and take time to make your writing as effective as possible.

- Resist the urge to just plunge in. Remember to plan, plan, plan.

- If using an organizer, remember to record only 2 to 4 word phrases.

- *Never* copy directly from the book, the Internet, or any other source you have used—this is plagiarism.

- *Always* acknowledge or give credit to the sources you have used.

- If you are having trouble, consider changing your subject—keep going!

- When you do not have enough information, reassess whether you want to stick with the topic or select a new one with more information available.

- Rethink the topic—limit or narrow the subject.

- Rethink the topic—expand the subject.

- Be willing to give up parts: specific facts that don't fit with the topic.

- Use interesting facts. They will give you authority as a writer.

- Don't be afraid to change your ideas around.

- Spend time and thought on the lead or first line—it is important.

- Think about your title last and provide it.

© 2007 *Reclaiming Reluctant Writers* by Kellie Buis. Permission to copy for classroom use. Pembroke Publishers.

Eyewitness Organizer

Template with prompts to be determined by teacher or student

Purpose: _____

Audience: _____

Genre: _____

Topic—Universal: _____

Topic—Specific: _____

On each horizontal line below, a prompt or heading to help organize student writing in a specific genre may be given.

_____   _____   _____

_____   _____   _____

_____   _____   _____

_____   _____   _____

© 2007 *Reclaiming Reluctant Writers* by Kellie Buis. Permission to copy for classroom use. Pembroke Publishers.

_____   _____   _____

_____   _____   _____

Companion Poem:

Hook/Lead/Opening sentence: Start with action, a question, dialogue, an interesting fact, a strong opinion, or a single word.

_____

_____

Concluding Sentence: _____

_____

Good Title: _____

© 2007 *Reclaiming Reluctant Writers* by Kellie Buis. Permission to copy for classroom use. Pembroke Publishers.

6: The Need for Shared Responsibility

I know that Adam has a kinesthetic intelligence that displays itself in his devotion to skateboarding and snowboarding. He has little time for the sedentary act of writing or little interest in cleaning up his writing. From the physical act of forming letters on the page to the mental act of sifting and sorting his thoughts into complete sentences let alone thinking about the conventions and presentation of his writing, this task has never been easy for Adam.

I also know that Adam is as inquisitive as he is active. I decide to try to channel Adam's strong sense of curiosity into helping him overcome some of the difficulties and lack of patience he has as a writer. Adam has recently developed a fascination with the explosion of the Hindenburg from some nonfiction reading done at home with his dad.

I create news reporting eyewitness organizers to connect the students, especially reluctant writers such as Adam, to the universal topic of natural or man-made disasters. Doing so gives Adam some direction for his choice of writing topic, yet affords him room to choose a specific topic within the universal one.

Adam proves to be a keen historian, spending time at home exploring and recording his newfound knowledge about the explosion of the Hindenburg. It is the first time that I have seen Adam eager to revisit his writing. He is prepared to take the time to revise his news story and to willingly consult a scoring guide to improve it. He is motivated to check the conventions of his text and reminds the peer editor that he needs a conference to finalize the changes he has made. He is equally keen to prepare a multi-media presentation, quickly organizing a writing exhibition to share his vast knowledge and the famous media clip of the Hindenburg's fiery final moments.

The students admire Adam for the vast knowledge he shares about the demise of the Hindenburg. Adam has made a strong connection with writing as a purposeful learning activity. Much more exacting in his writing than usual, he has done a good job of cleaning up his text, making it readable by following conventional standards. He has also made a strong connection with his peers. His mother sends a note, thanking me for her son's renewed enthusiasm about coming to school.

So far, we have taken great care to introduce our reluctant writers to free flow personal writing (notebooks) and organized public writing (eyewitness organizers). We have nurtured good attitudes and fluency. We have routinely modeled talk about text through read-alouds and write-alouds, revision included. Our reluctant writers have spent lots of time writing. They have spent lots of time planning. At last, we can challenge them to revisit their writing a number of times—we are ready to introduce them to revising and editing their work.

We are getting closer and closer to formally engaging them in writing as revision and in paying close attention to conventions. We also acknowledge that editors—teachers and peers—will help them with this part of the writing process. We are careful to invest time and energy into making these experiences positive for them by acknowledging what they have done well and working on improving one trait at a time.

This chapter explores the challenge of introducing our reluctant writers to the heart of writing: rewriting. It urges us to share the responsibility with them as peer editors using scoring guides to assess, revise text, and reformulate their writing goals and the writing goals of others. We begin this challenge to reclaim reluctant writers with a review of myths and realities related to five critical success factors clustered under the need for shared responsibility and then discuss each of these factors:

- the need to assess for learning
- the need for writing as rewriting
- the need for revising and editing to be social
- the need to keep what is important
- the need for computer-based learning

Using Assessment for Learning

Myth: Teachers have been taught how to properly assess and evaluate writing. Teachers find scoring guides and rubrics useful to teach the traits of good writing to reluctant writers.

Reality: The essential traits of good writing can be mastered through routine use of checklists and scoring guides, yet many teachers don't believe in them, or if they do, they don't use them enough for there to be an impact on the quality of their students' writing. After being explicitly taught how to use scoring guides, reluctant writers make dramatic improvements in their writing through their own assessment and evaluation practices. The most significant improvements result from mini-lessons that include explicit explanations, exemplars, and practice with various rubrics or scoring guides (as applied to read-alouds and write-alouds).

Challenge: Engagement is reduced to its lowest level for reluctant writers when they have no hope of moving their writing forward, when they lack feedback and knowledge of revision and editing practices to improve it. How do we infuse the positive use of scoring guides into our teaching of writing?

Meeting the Need

This critical success factor is about nurturing revision and editing practices through the use of scoring guides in the hands of our students during read-alouds and write-alouds. Our challenge is to teach our students how to use them to assess writing so they may properly revise text. It demands that they understand the criteria and the specific language related to writing assessment and evaluation.

We formally introduce our reluctant writers to assessment when we model the use of scoring guides on what they *hear* during read-alouds (ideas, sentence fluency, voice, and words) and what they *see* during write-alouds (organization, conventions, and presentation). Our students take delight in assessing the writing of well-known authors that they hear during read-alouds and even greater delight in assessing the writing of their own teacher that they see during write-alouds. Read-alouds of well-crafted texts in specific genres give writers wonderful exemplars of each trait of writing; they help writers know where they need to go in their writing.

We set high expectations for our writers when we explicitly showcase what a 5 means on a scoring guide:

Ideas: The text makes sense, seems really clear, and gets the message across.
Organization: The text has smooth transitions from the beginning to the end; it all fits together and is easy to follow.
Voice: The text reveals the voice of the writer; the writer speaks right to the audience, with the power to make readers laugh or cry.
Word Choice: The text has clear words that paint a picture; they are the best words to say what the writer wants to say.
Sentence Fluency: The text has an easy-to-read sound, and the sentences have a comfortable rhythm to them when said out loud.
Conventions: The punctuation makes the reading glide, and the grammar contributes to the style of the piece.
Presentation: The text is clear, easy to read, and looks finished.

"Text Scoring Guide," a reproducible scoring guide based on these descriptions, appears at the end of this chapter.

We model how to revise and edit text for everyone. No one is left out of this important training as the students will consult the same criteria during peer conferences and student-led exhibitions (see Chapter 7). But for now, we confine our initial practice with assessment criteria to the writing of distant others; we will not assess the writing of the students until they are ready to share writing at their student-led exhibitions and are familiar and well prepared with the criteria for scoring the text they take public.

Exemplars of students from other years can be used to give students some good exposure to the criteria they will be using to take their own writing public in the near future. Students love to hear the writing of other students they may know through school or siblings. These students see and hear that other students are appreciated as authors.

Our intention is to instill a positive attitude towards assessment in our writers. We infuse the language of writing criteria into our read-alouds and write-alouds, and encourage students to view revision and editing practices as natural. We begin this challenge by having them hear and see us work with the criteria of plain scoring guides, such as those on pages 60 and 90, or any others from our school districts. We most often specifically assess one trait, but on rare occasions, may address all six key writing traits plus presentation. For most students it is best to develop one trait at a time. As students become more familiar with each trait and from read-alouds and write-alouds develop a good working knowledge of what effective writers do, we may decide to assess some of our students for all traits on one rubric.

When students assess the writing of others, they gain a better grasp of criteria to apply to their own writing and that of their peers. They consider ideas, organization, voice, word choice, sentence fluency, conventions, and presentation.

William Zinsser reminds us that "the essence of writing is rewriting" (1988, 15).

Checklists and scoring guides are useful, reasonable tools in the hands of all our writers. We invite the students to score read-alouds and write-alouds as leadership opportunities for previously bored, underpowered writers. When our most reluctant writers are given the role and responsibility—the power—to assess the teacher's writing in front of their peers, they most often rise to the occasion. They surprise everyone! When given the role and responsibility to assess the writing of their peers, they become positively empowered members of the writing community.

Recognizing Writing as Rewriting

Myth: Rewriting is a sign of failure. People who know how to write get it right the first time.

Reality: Reluctant writers have the mistaken belief that good writers get it right the first time and that only poor writers "tinker" with drafts over and over again. Teachers tend to support this belief by allowing some reluctant writers "out" of the writing process at this critical point. Rewriting is, however, the essence of what we do as writers and crucial to the development of reluctant writers. It becomes our major emphasis when we have their trust, when we are confident that they are ready, willing, and able for this new challenge. They will learn more and improve their writing more through receiving feedback on it. Teachers need to model appropriate feedback for rewriting and keep their reluctant writers *in* the process if they are to meet with success.

Challenge: Engagement is reduced to its lowest level for reluctant writers when they attempt to write text while focusing on the paper's final form, short-circuiting the writing process. How do we develop their belief that feedback for rewriting is an essential part of their writing process?

Meeting the Need

Shift in Teaching Practice
We can provide early feedback to writers to focus rewriting efforts.

This challenge is about patiently teaching our reluctant writers to take a different view of the writing process. It is critical that our writers participate in more and more writing, rewriting, feedback, and assessment in order to move from drafts to final copies and from reluctant writers to competent writers.

Reluctant writers will spend less time rewriting when they work hard to organize their thoughts on their organizers. Our writers will be much more successful if we structure time to review the work done on their organizers. We offset some difficulties almost before they occur by having brief conferences to review their progress at critical junctures. When the organizer is finished to their satisfaction, they book a time to review it with us or with a peer editor. We check the organizer to determine their areas of strength and weakness and give them guidance and feedback on any struggles they may be having. We remember to be consistent in using the language common to our checklists, scoring guides, and write-alouds so the students are familiar with this when they revise and edit the work of peers or talk during their student-led exhibitions.

Feedback to our writers begins with identifying things they are doing well and one or two areas for improvement. We compliment our writers with informative comments to foster self-efficacy without the use of rewards. We take time with the writers to ask them how they feel they are doing. We show interest in what they have done well and what they can work on. We are sincere and specific in the praise we give. We want to make sure that our comments are respectfully directed towards the writing, not the writer.

Sincere and Specific Feedback: Examples

Ideas: Your ideas are fresh and original. I was so engaged in this story that I didn't want to put it down!

You have an important idea here. Can you slow down this part of the text by writing more?

The character is becoming believable. Is there another gesture or action that would show who your character truly is?

Is there more than one story here? Let's find your one story. What is your favorite part? Can we build on that?

Organization: This is an inviting first line. It starts with action that pulls me as the reader into the story!

Each paragraph of the text fits together and is easy to follow.

Voice: Your personality as a writer shines through—I knew your purpose and feeling as a writer throughout your story!

This is a carefully crafted last line. It ends the story well.

Word Choice: "Turbulent" was a strong word for this line! I could feel its power—it seemed to be just right!

This word paints a picture for me.

Sentence Fluency: These sentences have such rhythm to them. They roll off my tongue. I didn't stumble once!

You have a good variety of sentences—some long, some short; this writing really flows.

Conventions: Thanks for thinking of me as the reader.

Your writing was really easy to read! The punctuation helped me along.

Shift in Teaching Practice
We limit feedback to only a few suggestions at a time and train peer editors to do the same.

Ideally, we make only a few suggestions at a time, and preferably, these are related to one trait of the students' writing, such as ideas or fluency. Students need limited feedback quickly, with the opportunity to correct or revise the writing soon. At this stage in reclaiming our reluctant writers, it would be cruel to have them make all the changes that would make a perfect text. We train our students to work with editing and proofreading one aspect of the whole text. We typically give feedback related to one or two essential traits of writing.

Revising and Editing Among Peers

Myth: Peer editing is not a viable writing or learning activity. Teachers who feel this way may be uncomfortable about how to use scoring guides to give feedback to their writers; they may prefer to quietly conference with individual students about their writing progress.

Edit out loud. Listen to the music of the draft, and tune it so that each paragraph, each line, each word, each space between words creates a beat and a melody that supports and advances the meaning of the draft.
—Donald Murray

Reality: Many writers in Grades 3 to 9 are well able to revise and edit their work and the work of peers. They need not develop co-dependency with the teacher.

Revising text, however, needs to be a shared, highly social activity. Most writers prefer a noisy exchange of ideas with peers to sitting quietly at desks revising their own texts. We cannot underestimate the importance of the social, active dimension of revising and editing practices. When students work together, their knowledge grows. When they share the role of peer editor, they make better judges of their own work and lessen the teacher's load. They benefit greatly from the shared responsibility of writing community members to give feedback on ideas, organization, voice, word choice, and sentence fluency for their texts. To become skilled at revising will be a lengthy process and require lots of support and encouragement from the teacher and other mentors in the class. Writing alone is neither easy nor necessary.

Challenge: Engagement is reduced to its lowest level for reluctant writers when there is no hope for them to be social and active in giving and getting feedback. How do we make revision and editing a shared responsibility?

Meeting the Need

It is critical to the success of reluctant writers that they become empowered responsible editors. When they become editors, they become better writers. Practice makes perfect. When they edit work in a particular genre, they become learners of that genre. We need to believe our classes are filled with capable editors worthy of being empowered to have a shared responsibility to assess their own writing and the writing of their peers.

Students who are comfortable or expert at revising and editing independently become the peer editors who oversee four or five writers individually, as needed. We empower three to six students to become editors working with writers to guide them and answer their questions and concerns. Editors can see their teacher, in role as editor-in-chief, about any questions or concerns they have about their role.

Serving as an editor can become one of the most sought after and engaging roles during open writing sessions, and students take the job seriously. We provide a special place for peer conferencing and have our peer editors sit at certain desks and wear special badges to signify their role. We equip them with an Editing symbol chart, scoring guides, checklists, and ink stamps to indicate Draft, Revised, or Proofread—the pen, however, is held by the writer throughout. We set out a schedule of times the designated peer editors are available to meet with any of their writers to offer suggestions. Times for conferencing are subject to peer editors revising and editing their own work first.

Sample Peer Conferencing Schedule		
Time	**Peer Editors**	**Writers**
Tuesday	Hannah	Sam, Sarah, David, Tavleen, Tarin
Wednesday	Kevin	Anna, Brandon, Leilah, Jessica, Amanda
Thursday	Meagan	Curtis, Blake, Alan, Courtney
All times are during open writing session.		

We are careful to select the best students for this role: not necessarily the best writers. The most workable peer editor–writer relationships are those with stu-

Prompts for Editors to Use with Writers
I like the way you . . .
You made me think about . . .
Tell me about this . . .
I noticed you . . .

Shift in Teaching Practice
We create a special place where peer conferences about writing can occur, empowering a few students to guide others.

Suggested Symbols

I?	Ideas
O?	Organization
P△	New paragraph
Frag	Sentence fragment
Fl	Fluency
RO	Run on sentence
WC	Word choice

Conventions:

Sp	Spelling
C	Capital letter
O	circle with convention in it: insert
Ø	circle with a line through it: delete

dents who are close in writing development, with the peer editor being slightly ahead of the writer. Typically, our strongest writers do not do well with our weakest writers. When low functioning students select to work with high functioning students, tension can be created, reducing the quality of the interaction. ELL students can make significant progress when they pair up with students they want to be with. Many of our best peer conferences come from students requesting to work together. When given this leadership role, reluctant writers may become some of the best peer editors. Peer editors must be committed to taking this role of shared responsibility with the teacher seriously.

We teach peer editors to be respectful of the writers and not to judge them. (See the handout "Modelling Peer-Conferencing Skills and Behaviors" on page 91.) Editors need to talk in terms of the writing, not the writer. Our open writing sessions should be full of lots of healthy, respectful, and at times, noisy conversation. Peer editors can be encouraged to consider the following questions after a conference:

- Was I helpful?
- Did we take turns speaking?
- Did I offer guidance—or take over the conference?
- Did I assess only the trait I agreed to assess at the beginning of the conference?
- Did I wait patiently and not interrupt the writer's conversation?
- Did I actively listen to the writer?
- Did I use gestures, expression, and posture to look interested?
- If any moment got tense or negative, what did I do?

Seeing Conventions as Tools to Clarity

Myth: Learning conventions of print is an important part of the writing process for reluctant writers. Teachers need to be concerned with the teaching of grammar, spelling, and punctuation.

Reality: Research confirms that the formal teaching of grammar, spelling, and punctuation has no benefit on elementary students' writing (Chapman 1997, 191). Not only does it promote negative attitudes towards writing, it takes writers away from useful ways to improve their grammar, spelling, and punctuation.

Reluctant writers learn to spell best by writing; they do not work well in formal spelling programs, especially those with spelling tests. Teachers make these already anxious writers more defeated when they spend unnecessary hours on formal instruction, such as practice with spelling lists. This kind of formal instruction negatively affects their attitudes towards words and interferes with the development of their fluency and independence as writers. These programs are neither relevant nor important to reviving our reluctant writers' desire to write well.

Challenge: Engagement is reduced to its lowest level for reluctant writers when they are led to believe that writing equals spelling plus grammar plus punctuation. How do we provide opportunities for students to see the power of conventions to add clarity to a text without making them a formal study?

How We Peer-Conference
We care about who we are as writers.
We talk about the writing, not the writer.
We are respectful. We make no judgments.

Shift in Teaching Practice
We need to emphasize that revising, with its focus on meaning, is important and be sure not to confuse it with editing, which tends to be associated with the mechanics of writing.

Answering the Big Five Questions can add to a text's meaning, clarity, and overall strength. Writers can ask these questions of themselves before a conference with the teacher or peer editor, or they can be prompted by the teacher or peer editor at a conference. The intent is to improve the ideas, organization, voice, word choices, and sentence fluency of the writing.

Writers' ideas are important.

Meeting the Need

This critical success factor is about designing writing action plans centred on the development of ideas, organization, voice, sentence fluency, word choice, conventions, and presentation, not just on conventions of print. There is little room in a plan to reclaim reluctant writers through formal instruction in grammar, spelling, and punctuation. Our challenge is to teach these skills primarily through eyewitness organizer writing with a focus on drafting to clarify meaning for the reader. Although these skills are considered part of the revising and editing processes (because they contribute to text meaning), they are more closely related to read-alouds, write-alouds, and student-led exhibitions, where we talk about them as tools of the author to help the reader navigate the text.

We teach our writers that revising and editing are separate, distinct stages to make their writing more effective as well as correct. We teach them to first respond to the ideas, not the mechanics of the writing. We model how to consider meaning rather than correctness when we read aloud to them (*they hear this*). We model how to consider the correctness of the text when we write aloud (*they see this*). We demonstrate our concern for ideas and the meaning of the text by having our peer editors work with these five revising strategies, expressed in terms of questions.

- **Adding:** What words, phrases, and sentences can you add?
- **Substituting:** What words, phrases, and sentences can you substitute?
- **Rearranging:** What words, phrases, and sentences can you rearrange?
- **Combining:** What phrases and sentences can you combine?
- **Deleting:** What words, phrases, and sentences can you delete?

Revising through questions

Some examples of the kinds of revision practices we expect our students to use in conferences, on their own, and during write-alouds are outlined here. These practices are intended to strengthen how writers respond to the meaning of text.

Adding: "What do we need to add to make this text more interesting and informative?"

Text: *She watered the garden.*
Revision: *When she watered the Lady's Mantle beads of water hung on the leaves like perfect little tear dropped jewels.*

Good writers include interesting information in their texts, demonstrating their expertise or knowledge. When specific details, such as *beads of water hung on the leaves like perfect little tear dropped jewels,* are included, credibility is given to the text and author.

Adding: "What do we need to add to make this text more interesting and informative?"

Text: *The dog howled.*
Revisions
Add time: *Last night, the dog howled.*
Add size: *Last night, the enormous dog howled.*
Add place: *Last night, the enormous dog howled outside my window.*
Add person: *Last night, the neighbor's enormous dog howled outside my window.*

Good writers provide detailed information in the text. Students need to know how writers supply details or topic knowledge to the text. When specific details, such as time, size, color, and name, are added, the text has greater authority.

Adding: "Can we add phrases or sentences to improve the description of the story setting and use striking language? Here's an example of what I mean from *Charlotte's Web* by E. B. White: 'It smelled of hay and it smelled of manure. It smelled of the perspiration of tired horses and the wonderful sweet breath of patient cows. It had a sort of peaceful smell—as though nothing bad could happen ever again in the world.'"

Good writers tell parts of their stories through description. Students need to realize how writers such as E. B. White include descriptions of the smells in their stories rather than just telling the stories. Students can learn how and when to add description and striking language to their stories.

Writers' organization of text is important.

Adding: "What sentences can we add to this dialogue to move the story forward?"

Text: *"What will we do?"*
"What do you want to do?"
"What do you think?"
"What do you think?"
"Should we go out tonight?'
"Do you mean sneak out?"
Revision: *"So it is agreed. We will sneak out of the house tonight."*

Good writers are careful to use dialogue to move their stories forward so students need to see demonstrations of the proper use of dialogue. Students can learn how to be economical with their dialogue.

Adding: "What sentences can we add to the parts of the story that matter the most so that we can slow these important parts down?"

Text: *Suddenly Theresa fell off her horse and was lying on the arena floor.*
Revision: *Final thrust and takeoff! Bam! Contact—hoof to wood. The top pole rattled and wobbled loose as the horse and rider tumbled forward helplessly. Dust doused the pair as they sprawled on the arena floor. Silence loomed over the crowd. Snuffles and snorts from the fallen horse echoed his surprise as he instinctively righted himself. Theresa lay still—caught in her own unexpected moment of confusion, serious and silent.*

Good writers know when and how to slow the text down. Students need to know how to slow down the important parts through the addition of sentences that provide a more detailed picture in the minds of the readers. Adding sentences shows that we are not content as writers to just tell the story, but to slow the action down and showcase important moments.

Writers' word choices are important.

Adding: "What word can we add to make this writing better?"

Text: *The captain cried out to force the buccaneers back from whence they came.*
Revision: *"Avast!" cried out the captain to force the buccaneers back from whence they came.*

Good writers demonstrate knowledge about their subject. Students need to know how writers add particular words to improve their texts and share special knowledge of their subjects. *Avast* is a nautical term meaning to stop or cease, a good addition to this pirate story to help it ring true. Students can learn to find such words through a thesaurus search.

Writers' voice is important.

Adding: "What sentences can we add to improve the mood or feeling of this story?"

Text: *I went to the haunted house. I stood at the broken down gate. I went through and climbed the stairs. I entered the house. Inside I saw . . .*
Revision: *I went to the haunted house. I stood at the broken down gate. Sweat gathered on my forehead. My heart thumped louder and louder as I climbed the stairs. Fear gripped my throat, halting my breath and making me feel too weak to proceed or turn back.*

Good writers convey feelings and thoughts to their stories to give them more life; otherwise, stories may be just lists of events and offer little writers' voice. Students need to see the importance of including feelings to give life to their stories—emotions can set the mood and develop the meaning of the text.

Writers' word choices are important.

Substituting: "Can we substitute a word here to improve this text?"

Text: *They were happy. They knew they would always love one another.*
Revision: *They were blissful. They knew they would always love one another.*

Good writers are careful to select exactly the right words for their texts. Students need to see how authors might make substitutions for "choice" vocabulary in sentences to enhance the meaning of the text. *Happy* may be an overused word; *blissful* seems to be just the right word in the selection.

Writers' voice is important.

Substituting: "Can the words we write improve the voice of the text? . . . Here's an example where unusual words make a difference: '*You surely is not telling me that a little whizzpopping is forbidden among human beans?*' It's from *The BFG* by Roald Dahl."

Good writers are careful to select exactly the right voice for their texts. A voice may be silly, thoughtful, cantankerous, passionate, caring, frightening, funny, timid, delightful, gracious, clever, childlike, academic, pleasing, flat, mean, or mysterious. Students need to see how authors select "choice" vocabulary in sentences to enhance the voice or set the mood of the text. Roald Dahl's selection of "whizzpopping" and "human beans" give some sense of childlike delight to his character (and his story) of the BFG, Big Friendly Giant.

Writers' ideas and related word choices are important.

Substituting: "Can we substitute a new name to contribute to the authenticity of the character?"

Text: *Buttercup lurched violently at the villainous creature.*
Revision: *Bracken lurched violently at the villainous creature.*

Good writers breathe life into their characters. Students need to know how writers determine the right names for their characters. Appearance, manners, expressions, and name need to somehow match. Substituting the name Bracken for Buttercup contributes to the showing (rather than just telling) of what kind of a character this is—a superhero! Consistency helps.

Writers' word choices and fluency are important.

Substituting: "Can we substitute a different noun or pronoun to replace a noun to vary our sentence beginnings? Doing that would better hold the interest of the readers."

Text: *The raccoons were eating our garbage.*
Possible revisions
These saucy creatures . . .
These beggars . . .
They . . .
These omnivores . . .

Good writers substitute words to give variety to their sentences. Students need to see how writers use a number of different sentence beginnings. Substituting a different noun or pronoun contributes to the fluency of the text.

Showing ideas or implying them is important.

Substituting: "Can we substitute a phrase or sentence to contribute to showing rather than telling this story?"

Text: *He was afraid.*
Revision: *Again he dropped the pen. Once he picked it up, he squeezed it and twisted it in his hands.*

Good writers show rather than simply tell their stories. Students need to see how writers show rather than tell, too. Students can learn how the boy is afraid by how he drops and holds his pencil rather than by the author simply writing that he is afraid.

Substituting: "Can we substitute a phrase or sentence to contribute to implying rather than telling this story?"

Text: *The boys had fun.*
Revision: *The boys got up before their Dad and had this terrific breakfast—leftover pizza and chocolate cake."*

Good writers imply rather than tell their stories to add interest to them. Students need to see how writers imply some of the information in their stories rather than just telling them. In the above revision, students can note how the boys had fun in a less obvious way than if the author announced it.

Writers' organization is important.

Rearranging: "Can we rearrange the sentences in this text to start with action rather than details of the story?"

Text: *Once there was a very brave young boy named Jet. He desperately needed to find out what lay ahead in the cave. He stood at the entrance and listened intently. A scream echoed across the space. Although he thought himself a brave boy he lacked the courage at this particular moment to challenge the sound with his own voice.*
Revision: *A scream echoed across the closed cave. Jet stood at the entrance and listened intently for a repeat of the sound. Although he thought himself a brave boy he lacked the courage at this particular moment to challenge the sound with his own voice.*

Good writers get to action quickly at their story beginnings—the revision brings the reader right into the text. Students need to know how authors rearrange their sentences to start with action and then move to provide the background details of the text soon after this.

Combining: "Can we combine these sentences to improve the fluency of this text?"

Text: *Shopping is fun. Especially with my friend.*
Revision: *I especially like to go shopping with my friend.*

Good writers typically write in complete sentences. Students need to know how authors combine words in several sentences to improve text meaning and fluency.

Writers' fluency is important.

Combining: "Can we combine some sentences to ensure that the writing is not flat with the sentences that are all the same length?"

Text: *I love riding horses. It is fun to ride. I like to ride pintos. Riding ponies is fun too.*
Text: *Riding rocks! It is so much fun to go riding, I just love it. I like to ride pintos but I like to ride ponies too!*

Good writers vary their sentence lengths. Students need to see how combining simple sentences allows writers to create a variety of sentence kinds and lengths, which avoids flat, boring writing.

Connecting: "Can we use words to help us connect our ideas between sentences?"

- We can use location words: above, amid, beneath, in back, beyond, close to, in front of, next to, beside, by, between.
- We can use compare/contrast words: similarly, however, conversely, even so, otherwise, even though, but.
- We can use time words: first, second, third, next, later, then, afterward, soon, after a while, after that, in the meantime, presently, in time.
- We can use concluding words: finally, to sum up, to clarify, as a result, in summary, in conclusion.
- We can add information with these words: besides, in addition, for example, further more, equally important, thus.

Good writers need to learn how to connect ideas in one sentence to the ideas in the next sentence, and one paragraph to the next, as well.

Writers' word choices are important.

Deleting: "What word should be deleted because it is unnecessary and does not contribute to the text?"

Text: *I quickly scanned the room.*
Revision: *I scanned the room.*

Good writers are precise with the meanings of the words. Beginning writers can be wordy so students need to see how a writer may be using two words that say the same thing. Students should learn that if a word does not have a purpose in a sentence, it can be deleted—*quickly* is unnecessary if we understand scanning to mean looking quickly.

Equations of Writing

Ideas + Fluency + Voice = Powerful writing

Spelling + Punctuation + Grammar≠ Powerful writing

We *revise* our ideas, organization, sentences for fluency and length, and word choice.

We *edit* our usage of conventions and presentation of the final copy of our writing.

Two useful spelling resources are *Making Words Stick* by Kellie Buis and *Word Savvy* by Max Brand.

Color Code Editing

Writers and peer editors may find it helpful to color-code

• short, medium, and long sentences
• ideas that match in each paragraph
• punctuation
• topic and concluding sentences

Color-coding text allows students who are weak or less than interested in taking the time to self-assess their writing to systematically go through the text. Many students like to color-code because they can more clearly see sentence length and overuse or not enough use of punctuation.

Learning conventions in a writing context

Only after a piece of writing has undergone application of these strategies do we concern ourselves with editing or with correcting mechanical errors. We make a shift in our teaching practice to release our reluctant writers from the bonds of spelling and punctuating to be appreciated as good authors (see Classroom Banners, given in the margin). We free them to write, knowing that their *ideas* are more important than the mechanics and that they will not be labeled as failures because they lack in these skills. They are then free to take risks with big words and play with their ideas in a way they never could if everything has to be correct. This is how we reclaim them.

Spelling Resources: These should be made available to our reluctant writers. Learning to spell is a developmental process that moves our writers towards conventional spelling. We can help our writers learn to spell by giving them easy access to

• mind maps or webs
• word lists and charts
• word walls, or visually displayed words usually classified in certain ways, for example, joining words, rhyming words, -*er* words, and compound words
• computer tools (grammar and spell checks, thesaurus, dictionary, and autocorrect function)
• brief reviews of strategies to spell, such as looking at a word and thinking about other words that may have the same pattern—knowing *sat* means you may know *bat, cat,* and *rat;* looking at a word part and thinking about other words that may have the same part and meaning—knowing *bio* means you may know *biology* and *biography;* thinking of another word that may provide a visual clue, then saying it, thinking about it, and writing it; and asking yourself which part of a word is right and which is wrong and writing it out

This is not to say that we do not teach spelling. It is the subject of mini-lessons for those students who need it. We gather groups of students together while other students are busy writing. We provide explicit instruction on word patterns or families, high-frequency words with irregular spellings, variant spellings (long vowels), and spelling strategies.

Although our writers benefit from some instruction, they do not need massive amounts of drill and practice. Something else to keep in mind is that hard copies of dictionaries tend to be of little value to reluctant writers: they lack the motivation to pick one up and use it, especially since they would have to have an idea of how the word is spelled anyhow. Many great writers today are well supported by editors and technology to overcome their challenges as spellers.

Punctuation: Much like spelling, punctuation is developmental. When students are eventually ready to present their writing publicly, they will have plenty of opportunities to see how punctuation conveys meaning. As students exhibit their writing, they model their use of punctuation in the context of authentic writing. During any student-led exhibition, it may be a good idea to offer a "Find the Mistake" challenge. Doing so gives everyone a chance to examine punctuation as an aid to understanding by the reader and to see that it is not a discrete skill.

Over time, students leading exhibitions provide the most powerful contextual teaching and discourse around the use of print conventions. In student-led exhibitions, authors engage the audience in grand conversations about the text that go well beyond the author sharing a text. Unlike Author's Chair, where writers share their writing by reading it aloud to the audience, student-led exhibitions are social, active teaching situations where the author talks with the audience—there is a transaction between the author and the audience—about the evolution of the text in terms of ideas, organization, voice, word choice, fluency, and conventions, and how effective they are or could be.

Incorporating Computer-Based Learning

Myth: Reluctant writers learn to write and go through the same writing phases as all student writers do.

Reality: Many of the difficulties experienced by our reluctant writers can be attended to on the computer. Technology enlivens writing practice. Software features boost word fluency. Web sites encourage publishing. Computer-supported learning can gently transform reluctant writers with severe language-based learning problems into master wordsmiths. When they become unencumbered by poor spelling or grammar, awkward sentence structure, illegible handwriting, and the like, they write more. Our goal is for reluctant writers to write for their own satisfaction.

Challenge: Engagement is reduced to its lowest level for reluctant writers when they have severe language-based learning difficulties that prevent them from getting their ideas down. How do we shift our practice to the use of computer-based learning to reactivate the intrinsic needs and desires of our most severely disabled writers to write?

Meeting the Need

Shift in Teaching Practice
We recognize the potential of computer tools to help our struggling writers overcome limitations.

This critical success factor is about enabling reluctant writers to more easily get their writing down with the use of computer-based learning. It demands that our reluctant writers be able to work with their topics and flow of ideas in a paperless environment. We don't force-feed them computer-based drill and practice of phonics games and activities. Instead, we give them access to software programs that help move them through their writing process as part of authentic writing practice.

We have many excellent computer tools and software programs that can put writing within reach for some students for the first time in their school careers. Students can hear the pronunciation of words in short audio clips at sites such as Merriam-Webster Online. Apple computers have a feature using highlighting of text on sticky notes on the desktop to activate the reading of the text in a voice selected in the menu, something that is especially helpful for students of limited language experience. The Google search engine has a translation section under its Language Tools feature that translates English into other languages and vice versa.

Word prediction is a powerful tool for the most reluctant writers who find writing even on a computer frustrating. Word prediction software reduces the number of keystrokes necessary for typing words. It gives students confidence that they can have access to the words they need and want to use. Students can generate personalized banks of words to be stored through a function in the menu of these programs. When they begin to write, they can access these words through the keystroke of the first letter—*b* would bring up *baseball* for a student with a sports background. The ability to create personalized predictive word lists is enormously helpful to them. The writing process becomes less cumbersome through personalized vocabularies.

We match reluctant writers with computer-assisted learning when they

- have severe expressive writing difficulties
- cannot write fast enough to keep pace with the flow of their ideas
- cannot retain ideas in their memories long enough to express them coherently
- have difficulties in handwriting due to limited fine motor skills (unless they have more difficulty keystroking)
- have difficulty expressing themselves orally
- have poor spelling skills
- have far better reading skills than expressive writing skills
- have word-finding problems

Jessica was as bright as a button and entirely verbal—a good talker but *not* a good writer. Jessica had a serious written output problem. She could not write nearly fast enough to keep pace with what she could think or say. Jessica was one of the few truly severely disabled writers I have encountered.

A portable word processor on Jessica's desk allowed her to close the gap between what she could think and commit to paper. It became her writer's notebook with eight files for her to work from and save to the class computer, where she could continue to use other software programs to support her writing. With the portable keyboard Jessica was better able to participate in our writing action plans.

"Text Scoring Guide," the reproducible page that follows, is a useful tool for student editors to apply to the writing of their peers and for members of the class generally to apply to read-alouds.

Once peer editors are in place to work with our reluctant writers to assess their writing, we are suddenly free of trying to push, pull, and cajole our most reluctant writers to be open to revision as part of good writing. We use scoring guides to help our reluctant writers look inward to nurture their understanding of what changes can be made to improve their genre writing. When we teach them to write stronger texts through the revising and editing processes, we are also suddenly free to look to the next big challenge: that of nurturing the presentation of their published writing.

Text Scoring Guide

Text: _____

Author: _____ **Editor:** _____

1 below expectations   2 developing   3 satisfactory   4 strong   5 exemplary

Ideas:	1	2	3	4	5

The text makes sense, is really clear, and gets the message across.

Organization:	1	2	3	4	5

The text has smooth transitions from the beginning to the end; it all fits together and is easy to follow.

Voice:	1	2	3	4	5

The text reveals the voice of the writer; the writer speaks right to the audience, with the power to make readers laugh or cry.

Word Choice:	1	2	3	4	5

The text has clear words that paint a picture; they are the best words to say what the writer wants to say.

Sentence Fluency:	1	2	3	4	5

The text has an easy-to-read sound, and the sentences have a comfortable rhythm to them when said out loud.

Conventions:	1	2	3	4	5

The punctuation makes the reading glide, and the grammar contributes to the style of the piece.

Presentation:	1	2	3	4	5

The text is clear, easy to read, and looks finished.

© 2007 *Reclaiming Reluctant Writers* by Kellie Buis. Permission to copy for classroom use. Pembroke Publishers.

Modelling Peer-Conferencing Skills and Behaviors

What We Model:

- Letting the writer hold the writing tool and keep control of it

- Asking how the writer is doing

- Establishing what you are talking about (if revising, which trait; if editing, which and how many conventions)

- Listening carefully and actively to what the writer says

- Asking how the writing process went (How did you make out with the writing?)

- Replying freely to any questions or concerns the writer may have (If the writer asks, "Do you like my word choices?" you could respond, "Some of them are fine, but others could use a little work.")

- Beginning with appreciation for a few positive aspects of the text—be specific ("I liked the . . .")

- Listening patiently so you won't interrupt the writer talking

- Looking interested—using gestures, expressions, and your posture to show you are interested in what you are both doing

- Giving constructive suggestions where needed ("How about trying to . . .")

- Remembering to discuss what you agreed to discuss—if it was revising, don't begin to edit it too.

- Giving reasons for the writer to consider your suggestions ("Sometimes when you read your text out loud you can hear the sentence fluency. When it slides off your tongue, it can sound really good.")

- Deciding what you agree on and what you disagree about in the text—sharing your opinions and ideas and being willing to "bend" on these if the writer comes up with better ideas

- Keeping to one or two traits of the writing to work on, unless the writer requests more conferencing

- Asking how the writer felt the conference went

- Considering, for yourself, how the conference went and what you could do to make the next one better!

© 2007 *Reclaiming Reluctant Writers* by Kellie Buis. Permission to copy for classroom use. Pembroke Publishers.

7: The Needs to Connect, Talk, and Celebrate

Two stuffed animals. A beautiful bunny. A well worn-out puppy. A lovely "before" family photo. Another photo of her brother with their dog. Not much room to work with these treasures on her desk. Kim somehow manages.

Both Kim's parents have died within a month of each other. Her mother first, of cancer, followed by her father of complications with his heart. Kim and I decided that her family could be with her during the school day . . . if it helps. She agrees. I surround her with a few of her most precious personal treasures and begin the work to help heal this deeply wounded little girl whose life, as she knows it, has vanished in her eighth year.

Where do I begin? How do any of us secure the essence of the important people, times, and treasures in our lives so that they will remain with us for the rest of our lives? We collect stories from the friends and relatives of Kim's family. Kim's mother's co-workers collect their memories into a beautifully bound book, tucked away for future reference. I also invite all the students to bring their most precious treasures to school—and they do!

Every space in the room is charged with energy. We have cleared the shelves as welcoming homes to all the stuffed animals, rocks, dolls, action figures, and tattered bits of some beloved baby blankets. We are all excited to see treasures that may well have been critical to the survival of some of these youngsters, whether it be navigating their first sleepover or trip to camp, or in Kim's case, remaining connected to her family. It is an engaging and exciting time as we roam around the class and share the tangled bits of our lives with one another.

The sharing of our personal treasures is a deeply meaningful writing action for these students. I invite the students to consider what language will best capture the audience's interest and enlighten members about their precious treasures. We talk about the importance of rich, colorful precise language that will most clearly, powerfully, and beautifully capture the essence of each item. I remind them to try to make pictures in the minds of the readers: pictures that exactly describe their treasures. I encourage them to focus on the details and the unusual aspects of their objects to convey not only their love of their treasures, but love of the language as well.

Kim is the first person to share her favorite treasure with the class. Her exhibition of her bunny is bittersweet. Kim is delighted to have everyone hear about her treasure and how he kept her company on many trips to the hospital to visit her mother. I am spellbound by the courage of this little girl as she shares her bunny story with the class. She has selected beautiful words to convey her attachment to this, her most prized, possession.

After all, in learning to write students get to make sense of the world, to weigh ideas, to explore values, to find their own conventions, to invent voice, styles, personae on the page—and then to test every thing out by communication with others, sharing writing, and exchanging responses.

—Harvey Daniels and Steve Zemelman, *A Community of Writers*, p. 3

Teachers who encourage their students to make choices, to take responsibility for their learning, to be independent and fulfilled in classrooms in which autonomy, decisiveness, risk-taking, and caring are recognized and appreciated know power shared is not lost—but increased. In a power struggle, on the other hand, someone always loses (Mamchure 1990).

This chapter is about nurturing our reluctant writers' connections with others through student-led exhibitions. Our challenge is to teach our students that writing is an act of communicating with an audience. Students present themselves as authentic authors formally sharing their prose and companion poetry with an audience during student-led exhibitions. In the culminating activity of each writing action plan, they are transformed from passive students to leaders, to teachers with power and control over the class. They are required to polish their writing and to speak publicly about it and the act of writing it for 20 to 30 minutes.

We address this specific challenge to reclaim reluctant writers with a review of myths and realities related to nurturing pride in presentation and discuss these five critical success factors:

- the need for power
- the need for connection
- the need to be heard
- the need to be authentic authors
- the need for celebrations

A Productive Kind of Power

Myth: The teacher holds the power of what students should know, care, and write about. Teachers, not students, have ownership of the learning. That is what reluctant writers believe, and to complicate this perception further, their teachers may believe that if students have power in the classroom, teachers lose it.

Reality: Reluctant writers feel they have nothing to write because they have come to the conclusion that writing has nothing to do with anything they are interested in. When reluctant writers are made to follow the topics and ideas of the teacher, they may complete the writing, but typically put forth less effort and offer a lower quality performance. Not inspired when the project does not satisfy their needs, they do not write with enough purpose to put forth their best effort.

When it comes to writing choices, it is not the teacher's job to make the decisions and hold all the power. When reluctant writers have control over their writing, they hold a productive kind of power, not the destructive kind that some of them are all too familiar with. These writers are typically easier to control when they have shared responsibility for the writing activities; hence, teachers have more power, too.

Challenge: Engagement is reduced to its lowest level for reluctant writers when they have no hope for ownership of their writing or learning, when they feel powerless in the classroom. How do we give power back to our reluctant writers?

Meeting the Need

This critical success factor is about giving ownership, leadership, and control of the class to our students through student-led exhibitions. Our challenge is to reverse the standard teacher-directed approach. We transform our reluctant writers from passive, powerless observers to active, powerful students-as-teachers. They become teachers for the 20 to 30 minutes of their writing exhibitions.

When we engage them as leaders with their exhibitions, we win over many reluctant writers.

Transforming the participation of reluctant writers from passive students to empowered teachers is critical to the revival of reluctant writers. When they exhibit their talents and interests in student-led exhibitions, they can see themselves as leaders and writers of worth. Student-led exhibitions provide a genuine opportunity for them to learn through leadership, to be empowered with their responsibility to fulfill the following important duties:

- to sign up for their exhibition times
- to prepare copies of their prose (front of 8.5 by 11 paper) and companion poetry (back of 8.5 by 11 paper) for each audience member
- to introduce themselves as authors
- to articulate their experiences as authors writing texts
- to read their prose in the given genre and companion poetry or have others read them
- to guide the readers through talk about their text (see page 98)
- to identify evidence of one or all of the essential traits of writing by highlighting the text for ideas, organization, sentence fluency, word choice, voice, conventions (viewed through the lenses of revising and editing), and presentation
- to identify ways to improve the text
- to reflect on their experiences as authors: what they know, wonder, and learned
- to share any artifacts or activities that go with their exhibitions (e.g., photos, models, movie clips, displays) or to introduce guests

Our role changes drastically as the writers assume leadership roles to share their writing exhibitions. Many reluctant writers will begin to find their voices as leaders and as mentors and gain influence over their peers. As they do so, we move gradually to the periphery of the learning, releasing responsibility. We are never, however, too far away and can lead from behind by

- responding to a situation, but only if necessary
- listening rather than talking
- standing back and assessing student performance
- helping individual students
- observing and assisting a leader or learners

Satisfying a Drive to Connect

Myth: Reluctant writers write to transmit their knowledge and the information they hold.

Reality: Reluctant writers are not as motivated to share information they have learned as much as they are to connect with their peers. They write for social reasons followed by the desires to communicate and make meaning. If students know that the writing activity will put them with their peers, they will typically come around to doing it. The social context is significant to facilitating reluctant writers to write.

Shift in Teaching Practice
We transform the nature of students' participation: they go from being passive students to empowered teachers.

Shift in Teaching Practice
As students discover their voices as writers, teachers lead from behind, providing support as necessary.

Schools can be environments where students satisfy this drive to connect and feel a sense of belonging. Building a spirit of connection and community is essential to creating a need-satisfying school characterized by high achievement.
—Bob Sullo, *Activating the Desire to Learn*, p. 8

Challenge: Engagement is reduced to its lowest level for many reluctant writers when they have no hope of connecting with others. How do we create situations for our reluctant writers to socialize through their writing?

Meeting the Need

This critical success factor is about honoring our reluctant writers' need to be with others. These writers may want to connect with their learning and their teacher, but it is far more likely that they want to connect with their peers. By including student-led exhibitions in our teaching practice, we allow writers to connect with others through their writing. These exhibitions play a significant role in enabling reluctant writers to take part in the writing community and reclaim themselves as part of it.

We nurture a powerful collaborative community of learners when members of the class have helping roles as part of student-led exhibitions. Peers enjoy contributing by

- handing out hard, or paper, copies of the text to be shared so students can follow along as the text is read aloud
- co-writing texts and then co-leading by sharing talk about the text
- working at the overhead on a transparency of the text
- circulating to help support students in highlighting the text for evidence of good use of ideas, organization, voice, sentence fluency, word choice, and conventions and in finding mistakes

The students exhibiting their work assign peer volunteers to fulfill needed tasks.

Shift in Teaching Practice
We promote students working together and supporting one another as they prepare for and present their student-led exhibitions.

Letting Voices Be Heard

Myth: Writers are motivated to write for marks, for the teacher, and maybe for parents. Writing is about "teaching" or communicating information they have learned and getting a mark for it.

Reality: Children work harder for authentic audiences than they do for grades. In many classrooms the teacher is the audience. If teachers change the audience to include other students, classes, or guests, they increase the students' interest to write. Even the most reluctant writers show enthusiasm at the prospect of being heard by an audience, perhaps for the first time in their lives. Anticipating the audience's reaction is one of the keys to successful writing.

Challenge: Engagement is reduced to its lowest level for many reluctant writers when they have no hope of sharing the stories that are important to them. How do we ensure that our reluctant writers have an audience so that their voices will be heard?

Meeting the Need

This critical success factor is about nurturing our reluctant writers by giving them audiences to share their best writing with. Our challenge is to ensure that our writers' voices will be heard. It demands that students polish the writing and lay claim to their voices by acting as authorities and speaking to their work as *authors* (a word that means to cause or create something). Harold Rosen reminds us, "Everyone has a story to tell." Our question is, Will our writers' stories be heard?

We set up student-led exhibitions so the students will share their treasures, collections, hobbies, and projects, and we give them the same importance that we give to mandated curricula. We give students time in school to shape inquiries around their treasures and interests, something that can become a motivating and interesting foundation for powerful personal and nonfiction writing and community building. The roots of nonfiction writing begin in our childhood fascinations with rocks, dinosaurs, skateboarding, hockey, dance, and more.

Our reluctant writers become more alert with invitations to present grand exhibitions of their personal interests, talents, artifacts, histories, memoirs, and family stories to their class. Student-led exhibitions are times for these writers to show who they are, what they like, or how clever they are. They bring out what is inside the students. We reclaim our reluctant writers when we provide invitations and opportunities for them to be passionate about what they know and to tell others.

Shift in Teaching Practice
We implement student-led exhibitions, where students have opportunities to talk about what matters to them and reveal something of themselves through their writing and related artifacts.

Popular Student-Led Exhibitions

- Scar stories—personal memoirs of accidents and trips to the hospital
- Autobiographies shared on the writers' birthdays
- Biographies where the subject of the biography visits the class
- Mysteries of science
- Reflective research (e.g., Why do we kill baby seals?)
- Sport demonstrations (e.g., hockey players, judo)

Oh no! Some of the ten-year-old girls were holding up the jockstrap from Steven's hockey bag with puzzled looks on their faces. Steven had just shared his hockey equipment and was passing it around the room as part of his student-led exhibition. Soon the puzzled looks turn into big smiles as this athlete/reluctant writer retrieved his equipment in return for hockey cards—his own hockey cards, complete with his picture, statistics, and signature. Some members of his hockey team arrived from other classes to assist Steven in his exhibition. The students listened attentively to his personal narrative and poetry on the trials and tribulations of training and playing the game. They were excited with the plan to complete his exhibition by going to the local skating rink that afternoon.

Steven had managed to become an engaged writer by doing what good writers do: writing on something he was passionate about. He wrote on what he cared about and what his friends cared about, too. He had an audience that was interested in his story and a new role in the school as a leader.

Other students followed Steven's example. Kevin decided then and there to write about his involvement with judo and invite the judo instructor to give the class a formal demonstration. Heather planned a cooking demonstration, Kyle an archery demonstration, and Emily a basketball demonstration.

What kid wouldn't be keen to imitate that kind of student-led exhibition?

Developing a Sense of Authorship

For me, it is essential that children are deeply involved in writing, that they share their texts with others, and that they perceive themselves as authors. I believe these three things are connected. A sense of authorship comes from the struggle to put something big and vital into print, and from seeing one's own printed words reach the hearts and minds of readers.

—Lucy Calkins, *The Art of Teaching Writing*, p. 9

Myth: Writing is easy for everyone except reluctant writers.

Reality: Writing is demanding for any writer, not just reluctant writers. It requires hard work, concentration, and a tolerance for frustration. Reluctant writers better understand what it means to be a writer when they share with others their experiences as writers, their successes and struggles, and their sense of authorship.

Challenge: Engagement is reduced to its lowest level for many reluctant writers when they believe writing is easy for everyone else but them. What can we do to support reluctant writers as they participate in the admittedly difficult authoring process?

Meeting the Need

This critical success factor is about authentic writing which begins when we acknowledge how difficult and rewarding writing is. It demands that we nurture the habit of mind needed to overcome what some students see as the adversity of writing, that we increase students' tolerance for frustration with this rigorous process. We must hold students' attention on how rewarding writing will be when they do their exhibitions. We must ensure that our students are referred to as authors and present as authors, and establish an atmosphere of care, respect, and interest in the writing they choose to share.

Typically, once upon a time, reluctant writers liked to showcase their writing; at some point, though, they become so self-conscious about the expression, neatness, punctuation, or spelling errors that they shun this. Many Grade 1 and Grade 2 students have wonderful stories they have written and proudly shared; however, soon enough they grow less concerned with their wonderful ideas and more sensitive to the need to be correct. When they determine it is more important to select short, guaranteed-to-be-correct words than risk spelling the words that best convey their meaning, the amount of text dwindles. Some resign themselves to dog stories instead of the dinosaur stories that filled their Grade 1 journals. Their favorite words shift from words that are important to them to words that are easier to write. Student-led exhibitions can return them to successfully showcasing their work and coming to know that good things come to those who write.

We use student-led exhibitions to empower writers to talk about their individual writing practice—what works for them as writers and what challenges them. When students explain writing to other students, we have a much better chance of engaging them. We use our time together to share new techniques they have tried in their writing. The student comment below addresses overcoming writer's block.

"I had writer's block," Kevin confessed to the class. "I just didn't know what to write. I talked to Mrs. Buis and she suggested I put the writing aside, work on something else for a while, or just take out time from my writing and read a good book. She gave me the idea to go back to my writer's notebook and take some time to think about entry points for my story as I lay in bed at night. Sure enough, the next day I had my ideas figured out and I was able to write this story. I used to have writer's block all the time and now I don't panic so much about it.

Shift in Teaching Practice
We promote peer assessment of students' writing, thereby engaging them during public exhibitions of writing.

I hear and I forget. I see and I remember. I do and I understand.
—Confucius

Most of us forget what we've learned in the last 48 hours. By teaching, you retain information longer and better. Teach your children and get them to teach you . . . To teach you, they must learn at a deeper level.

—Tim Cork, *Tapping the Iceberg*, p. 85

I know that some ideas will come to me if I try different things like waiting a day or checking out some other ideas I have in my notebook."

Leaders of student-led events invite other readers to talk about the text shown on the overhead. An important part of the talk about text is to engage the audience in finding evidence of good writing and evidence of improvements that could be made. Leaders have the choice of deciding to examine and talk about several aspects of the text. They can share the aspects they are most proud of and the ones that they can still work on.

One effective practice is to have leaders prompt students to use a variety of colored highlighters to identify various aspects. These include topic, main idea, details, clues to the genre (e.g., "Yours truly" as evidence of a letter), effective word choices and sentences, hard words, easy words, new words, interesting words, organization, voice, including mood and style, clear and confusing parts, fluency of text, transitions, and aspects of presentation, such as conventions of print. Students may also identify strong parts of the text, favorite parts, interesting ideas, and any aspects that could be strengthened. The text may lead them to wonder, to notice, to determine what they didn't like, and to consider what they learned. (See the reproducible "Reading as a Writer," page 101.) Students may read the text as respectful editors and as empathetic writers.

As observers to the student-led exhibitions, we are free to assist students to ensure that they are catching all they should about the writing or to complete assessments and evaluations of the students' writing and exhibitions. We can also decide to make informal observations of how the audience members engage in talk about text.

Celebrating What Our Authors Achieve

Myth: Reluctant writers know how to take credit and praise for the good work they have done as part of a class of authentic writers.

Reality: Reluctant writers often find it hard to be accepted and complimented in front of a group. For many, much of their writing time has been spent in remedial pull-out models with limited time to develop as authentic authors and to be acknowledged as authors.

Challenge: Engagement is reduced to its lowest level for many reluctant writers when their accomplishments in producing approximations of conventional text are not celebrated. How can we ensure that reluctant writers are praised specifically and sincerely within the community of writers?

Meeting the Need

This critical success factor is about honoring the approximations our students make in any and all the essential stages of the writing process they have gone through. Our challenge is to continually move them towards conventional standards, recognizing that they have several years to refine their writing. We need to nurture our students' abilities to develop clarity and coherence without expecting a polished finished product. We need to remain process, not product, oriented, encouraging them to take risks and accept mistakes as part of how they learn. We must be respectful in the kind and amount of feedback we give them.

Shift in Teaching Practice
We enable students to share and celebrate memorable personal stories. A ritual is in place each day so that every writer's voice may be heard.

We must celebrate what the students have accomplished, not focus on what conventional standards they have failed to achieve. We must take time to celebrate every writer's successes.

Reluctant writers regain their capacity to learn when they go safely through the process of finding learning and are challenged to go deeper into their exploration of a topic—to do more than answer questions on a standardized test or partake in "memorize and spit it out" learning. With student-led exhibitions, writing is about students being mindful of their own ideas and stories. Reluctant writers need a venue—a time and a place—to share the important things they have to say. We want our students to be able to share their stories—whatever they may be—with integrity and joy!

In my classroom we have celebrated many memorable moments: moments I will not forget. Here are a few celebrations that have arisen out of student-led exhibitions:

- Jacquie's story about her brother and his recent death from leukemia
- Annie's experience with the Make a Wish foundation to go on a family trip to Disneyland
- Adam's display of a brand-new baby brother
- Kyle's sharing of a biography of his grandfather as a war veteran, with the guest appearance of his grandfather
- Steven's exhibit of his successes on a hockey team, with visits by five of his teammates in the school
- Heather's celebration of her Scottish heritage with traditional Scottish food that we made and ate together
- Kim's sharing of her mother's death from a serious illness
- Angela's sharing of her menagerie of pets from her family's pet store, all present at her exhibition (including a monkey!)
- Victoria's sharing of her doll which has been passed down through five generations
- Sam's sharing of his grandfather's uniforms and backpack from the First World War
- Brandon's sharing of the remodeling of his family's 1947 Packard, a car that his dad brought to school as part of the exhibition
- Jacquie's sharing of her Aboriginal heritage with a visit from her grandmother to perform a drum ceremony
- Sara's demonstration of her skill in judo, complete with a demonstration from her judo instructor

The reproducible page "Reading as a Writer" appears on the next page and can be used during student-led exhibitions. It is best for the teacher or a designated student to model how to complete it before students engage in the activity on their own.

In an enabling classroom environment where students work in partnership with the teacher, the tone is calm. The class is focused and relaxed with writers taking their leadership roles seriously at their student-led exhibitions. Behavioral issues disappear as reluctant writers revive the same kind of show and tell enthusiasm they first bounced into school with. Sharing the control, power, and responsibility with our reluctant writers to manage the teaching and learning of the writing community is one sure way to nurture all our students to write willingly and well, but especially, to reclaim our reluctant writers as responsive writers and revitalized students.

Reading as a Writer

Using your copy of the text being shared, think about the following, record some of your responses, and highlight the text itself, as appropriate.

Strong parts of the text

_____

_____

Favorite parts

_____

_____

Interesting ideas, word choices, and sentences

_____

_____

What I wonder about/What I noticed

_____

_____

What I didn't like

_____

_____

Problems or mistakes

_____

_____

Conventions of print

_____

_____

Clues to the genre

_____

_____

What I learned

_____

_____

© 2007 *Reclaiming Reluctant Writers* by Kellie Buis. Permission to copy for classroom use. Pembroke Publishers.

Appendixes

Strong Titles for Read-Alouds   *105*

This list identifies the titles and authors of texts that teachers may want to draw on for exemplary read-alouds. Listings span the genres of nonfiction; memoir; fictional narrative, including novels and picture and chapter books; and poetry.

Responding to a Read-Aloud Exemplar   *109*

These two reproducible pages provide one way in which students can respond to a text read aloud as an exemplar. Students are asked to think about content and ideas, text organization, word choice, and sentence fluency, and to provide examples and explanations.

Eyewitness Organizer with Sample Prompts Added   *111*

In an effort to better convey how teachers might work with an Eyewitness Organizer, sample headings are provided, along with annotations about organizer use.

Genre Lists: Searching for the Specifics   *113*

These nine pages outline possible headings related to various kinds of writing, including description, persuasion, character study, personal narrative, inquiry and exploration, biography and autobiography. The words and phrases can be applied to Eyewitness Organizers, as outlined in this resource, or they can be used to scaffold other student thinking, writing, and research. The intent is to help students find specific information. Although derived from classroom use, the ideas are suggestions only; they may be adapted freely.

Strong Titles for Read-Alouds

A text thoroughly enjoyed by a class one year may fail to engage a class the next year. That's why it's good to be able to draw from a wide range of options.

Nonfiction—Inquiry and Exploration

Air Is All Around You by Franklyn M. Branley
Animals That Glow by Judith Janda Presnall
A River Ran Wild by Lynn Cherry
Digging up Dinosaurs and Dinosaur Bones by Aliki
Flight: The Journey of Charles Lindbergh by Robert Burleigh
Force and Motion by Peter Lafferty
Fun with Light by Maria Gordon
Janice VanCleave's A+ Science Fair Projects by Janice VanCleave
Multicultural Cookbook for Students by Carole Albyn
The Popcorn Book by Tomie dePaola
Science Magic series by Chris Oxlade
Shipwreck at the Bottom of the World by Jennifer Armstrong
Sunken Treasure by Gail Gibbons
The Cloud Book by Tomie dePaola
The Complete Workbook for Science Fair Projects by Julianne Blair Bochinski
The Crocodiles Still Wait by Carol Carrick
The Magic School Bus series by Joanna Cole and Bruce Degen
The Science Book of Color by Neil Ardley
The Science Book of Light by Neil Ardley
The Science Book of Sound by Neil Ardley
The Science Book of Weather by Neil Ardley
The Scientific America Book of Greatest Science Fair Projects by Marc Rosner
The Way Things Work by David Macaulay
Trapped by the Ice by Michael McCurdy
Ukrainian Easter Egg Design Book by Luba Perchyshyn
Volcano by Patricia Lauber (about Mt. St. Helen's)

Biographies

Anastasia by Carolyn Meyer
Antarctica: Journey to the South Pole by Walter Dean Myers
Elizabeth I by Kathryn Lasky
Kaiulani by Ellen Emerson White
Lady of Chiao Kuo by Laurence Yep
Mae Jemison: A Space Biography by Della Yannuzzi
Nzingha by Patricia McKissack
On the Halfpipe with Tony Hawk by Matt Christopher

Riding Freedom by Pam Munoz Ryan
Terry Fox: His Story by Leslie Scrivener
Wright Brothers by Russell Freedman

Autobiographies

A Special Kind of Hero: Chris Burke's Own Story by Chris Burke
Bill Peet: An Autobiography by Bill Peet
Boy by Roald Dahl
Going Solo by Roald Dahl
Guts by Gary Paulsen
It's Not About the Bike by Lance Armstrong
I Was a Teenage Professional Wrestler by Ted Lewin
Knots in My Yo-Yo String by Jerry Spinelli
Michele Kwan: Heart of a Champion by Michele Kwan
October Sky (or *The Rocket Boys*) by Homer Hickam
Of Beetles and Angels by Asgedom Mawi
Rick Hansen: Man in Motion by Rick Hansen and Jim Taylor
The Game and the Glory by Michelle Akers (Soccer player)
The Great Muhammad Ali by Muhammad Ali
This Boy's Life by Wolfe Tobias
To Space and Back by Susan Okie

Memoirs

A Girl from Yarnhill by Beverly Clearly
An American Childhood by Annie Dillard
Angela's Ashes by Frank McCourt
A Road from Home: The Story of an Armenian Girl by David Kherdian
Autobiography of a Face by Lucy Grealy
Diary of Anne Frank by Anne Frank
Dove by Robin Graham
Gather Together in My Name by Maya Angelou
Grandfather's Journey by Cynthia Rylant
Hole in My Life by Jack Gantos
I Know Why the Caged Bird Sings by Maya Angelou
Into Thin Air by Jon Krakauer
I Was a Teenage Professional Wrestler by Ted Lewin
Knots in My Yo Yo String by Jerry Spinelli
Lakota Woman by Mary Crow Dog
Little House in the Big Wood by Laura Ingalls Wilder
Memories in Photographs by Lois Lowry
Miracle Man by Nolan Ryan
My Life in Dog Years by Gary Paulsen
No Pretty Pictures: A Child of War by Anita Loebel

Planet of the Blind by Stephen Kuusisto
Puppies, Dogs and Blue Northers by Gary Paulsen
Red Scarf Girl by Ji-li Jiang
Small Steps: The Year I Got Polio by Peg Kehret
The Abracadabra Kid: A Writer's Life by Sid Fleischman
The Keeping Quilt by Patricia Polacco
The Lost Garden by Laurence Yep
Thunder Cake by Patricia Polacco
'Tis by Frank McCourt
When I Was Nine by James Stevenson
When I Was Young in the Mountains by Cynthia Rylant
Woodsong by Gary Paulsen
Zlata's Diary: A Child's Life in Sarajevo by Zlata Filipovic

Fictional Narrative (Picture and Chapter Books)
A Boy, a Dog, and a Frog by Mercer Meyer
A Chair for My Mother by Vera Williams
Alexander and the Terrible, Horrible No Good, Very Bad Day by Judith Viorst
Amelia Bedelia by Peggy Parish
A Million Fish . . . More or Less by Patricia C. McKissack
A Necklace of Raindrops by Joan Aiken
Bedtime for Frances by Russell Hoban
Chicka Chicka Boom Boom by Bill Martin Jr.
Curious George by H. A. Rey
D. W. the Picky Eater by Marc Brown
First Tomato by Rosemary Wells
Freight Train by Donald Crews
Frog and Toad Are Friends by Arnold Lobel
Good Night, Gorilla by Peggy Rathman
Goodnight Moon by Margaret Wise Brown
Guess How Much I Love You by Sam McBratney
Harry and the Dirty Dog by Gene Zion
I Am a Bunny by Ole Risom
I Hear, I See, I Touch by Helen Oxenbury
Madeline by Ludwig Bemelmans
Make Way for Ducklings by Robert McCloskey
Mike Mulligan and His Steam Shovel by Virginia Lee Burton
Millions of Cats by Wanda Gag
Miss Nelson Is Missing by Harry Allard
Owen by Kevin Henkes
Petunia by Roger Duvoisin
Stevie by John Steptoe
Stellaluna by Janell Cannon
Swimmy by Leo Lionni
Sylvester and the Magic Pebble by William Steig
Ten, Nine, Eight by Molly Bang
The Berenstain Bears and the Spooky Tree by Stan and Jan Berenstain
The Cat Club by Esther Averill
The Snowy Day by Ezra Jack Keats

The Story of Ferdinand by Munro Leaf
The Sneetches and Other Stories by Dr. Seuss
The Stinky Cheese Man and Other Fairly Stupid Tales by Jon Scieszka
The Story of Babar by Jean de Brunhoff
The Story of Little Babaji by Helen Bannerman
The Tub People by Pam Conrad
Titch by Pat Hutchins
Where the Wild Things Are by Maurice Sendak
Whose Mouse Are You? by Robert Kraus

Beginning-middle-end books
3 Billy Goats Gruff by Glen Rounds
A Bad Case of Stripes by David Shannon
Armadillo Rodeo by Jan Brett
Brave Irene by William Steig
Cyrus the Unsinkable Serpent by Bill Peet
Doctor De Soto by William Steig
Fish Is Fish by Leo Lionni
How Droofus the Dragon Lost His Head by Bill Peet
Island of the Skog by Steven Kellogg
It's Mine by Leo Lionni
Little Loon and Papa by Toni Buzzeo
Paul Bunyan by Steven Kellogg
The Amazing Bone by William Steig
The Caboose Who Got Loose by Bill Peet
The Mitten by Jan Brett
The Mysterious Tadpole by Steven Kellogg
The Story of Ping by Marjorie Flack
Trouble with Trolls by Jan Brett

Fictional Narrative (Novels)
Adventure stories
Anne of Green Gables by Lucy Maud Montgomery
Emil and the Detectives by Erich Kastner
Encyclopedia Brown Shows the Way by Donald J. Sobel
Harris and Me by Gary Paulsen
Homer Price by Robert McCloskey
Kidnapped by Robert Louis Stevenson
Little House on the Prairie by Laura Ingalls Wilder
Pippi Longstocking by Astrid Lindgren
Ramona Forever by Beverly Cleary
Superfudge by Judy Blume
Tales of Fourth Grade Nothing by Judy Blume
The BFG by Roald Dahl
The Borrowers by Mary Norton

Animal tales
Black Beauty by Anna Sewell
Charlotte's Web by E. B. White
Find the White Horse by Dick-King Smith

Old Yeller by Fred Gipson
The Call of the Wild by Jack London
The Black Stallion by Walter Farley
The Red Pony by John Steinbeck
The Story of Doctor Doolittle by Hugh Lofting
The Tale of Peter Rabbit by Beatrix Potter
The Wind in the Willows by Kenneth Grahame

Fantasies
Peter Pan by J. M. Barrie
Redwall by Brian Jacques
The Hobbit by J. R. R. Tolkien
The Lion, the Witch and the Wardrobe by C. S. Lewis

Folk and fairy tales
Brer Rabbit and the Tar Baby retold by Julius Lester
"Cinderella" by Charles Perrault
The Jungle Book by Rudyard Kipling
The Little Prince by Antoine de Saint-Exupery
The Selfish Giant by Oscar Wilde
"The Ugly Duckling" by Hans Christian Andersen
Three Billy Goats Gruff by Asbjornsen and Moe

Incredible journeys
Alice in Wonderland by Lewis Carroll
A Christmas Carol by Charles Dickens
A Wrinkle in Time by Madeleine L'Engle
Charlie and the Chocolate Factory by Roald Dahl
The Chronicles of Narnia (series) by C. S. Lewis
The Return of the Twelve by Pauline Clarke
The Secret Garden by Frances Hodgson Burnett
The Wizard of Oz by Frank L. Baum
Treasure Island by Robert Louis Stevenson

Poetry
A Light in the Attic by Shel Silverstein
A Visit from St. Nicholas by Clement Clarke Moore
Falling Up by Shel Silverstein
Fly with Poetry: An ABC of Poetry by Avis Harley
"Jabberwocky" by Lewis Carroll
Joyful Noise by Paul Fleischman
Leap into Poetry by Avis Harley
Limericks by Michael Palin
The Random House Book of Poetry edited by Jack Prelutsky
Where the Sidewalk Ends by Shel Silverstein

Responding to a Read-Aloud Exemplar

Title: _____

Author: _____

Here is one example of something that I think is effectively written:

Features I noticed about this read-aloud:

I enjoyed the read-aloud: Yes or No

Why or why not? _____

_____

_____

It included what I wanted to know or was interested in: Yes or No

Explain: _____

_____

_____

It had features I liked: Yes or No

Example: _____

_____

_____

Ideas: It had ideas that appealed to me: Yes or No

Explain: _____

_____

_____

© 2007 *Reclaiming Reluctant Writers* by Kellie Buis. Permission to copy for classroom use. Pembroke Publishers.

Organization: I liked the ending: Yes or No

Explain: _____

_____

_____

Organization: I liked the first line or lead: Yes or No

Explain: _____

_____

_____

Sentence fluency: It had words, phrases, or sentences I liked: Yes or No

Example: _____

_____

_____

Word choice: I heard words I liked: Yes or No

Example: _____

_____

_____

It sounded the way it should: Yes or No

Explain: _____

_____

_____

© 2007 *Reclaiming Reluctant Writers* by Kellie Buis. Permission to copy for classroom use. Pembroke Publishers.

Eyewitness Organizer with Sample Prompts Added

Template with prompts to be determined by teacher or student

Purpose: To inquire about and explore a world culture

Audience: Class, teacher, parents

Genre: Non-fiction

Topic—Universal: Where in the World?—Know, Wonder, Learn, Research

Topic—Specific: [to be determined by individual student]

On each horizontal line below, a prompt or heading to help organize student writing in a specific genre may be given.

Where in the World? name, location	significance to you	landscape/physical features

[Although several pages of prompts appear as an index, it is expected teachers will adapt the prompts to suit their goals and student needs.]

special physical features—resources	special sights (unique, famous)	special sounds ?

[The prompts may seem basic, but experience has proven them to be most useful to reluctant writers.]

family/everyday life	special holidays	events/ceremonies

[To provide students with more room to manipulate words, be sure to increase template size to at least 8½ × 14 inch paper.]

customs—private and public	homes, incl. traditional	communication: languages

© 2007 *Reclaiming Reluctant Writers* by Kellie Buis. Permission to copy for classroom use. Pembroke Publishers.

traditional dress _____

faith and beliefs
taboos _____

special info _____

more special info _____

little known facts _____

other— _____

Companion Poem:

[Students may, of course, draft their poems on separate paper
or on the back of this form.]

Hook/Lead/Opening sentence: Start with action, a question, dialogue, an interesting fact, a strong opinion, or a single word.

_____

_____

Concluding Sentence: _____

_____

Good Title: [The student determines this last.] _____

© 2007 *Reclaiming Reluctant Writers* by Kellie Buis. Permission to copy for classroom use. Pembroke Publishers.

Genre Lists: Searching for the Specifics

These lists of headings will help young writers in their search for specific information they need in order to write effectively in a particular genre — as an example, students writing biographies need to search out important dates and events in a person's life. These lists are by no means fixed. We can amend the lists, adding or deleting information that students will use for their headings on Eyewitness Organizers. Younger, less able writers may work from a shorter list to gain experience at searching for specific information without feeling overwhelmed. We can challenge our more able students to work from comprehensive lists to search for more specifics.

How to Use These Genre Lists

There are many ways to work with the lists to improve our students' ability to conceptualize the specifics of a particular genre. Invite individual writers, partners, small groups, or the whole class to do any of the following:

- transfer a genre list, as is, onto their own Eyewitness Organizers as the headings of the specific information they will search for — or do the same for other writers
- decide for themselves which points on a genre list they will transfer onto blank Eyewitness Organizers to support efforts to organize ideas
- divide or jigsaw a list between several writers and share the information they find (For example, one student searches out important childhood dates and events of a famous person while another student searches out important adult dates and events.)
- create a genre list and then compare it to an equivalent that you, as the teacher, or other students have developed
- examine their finished texts to see that they have searched for all the specifics on their genre list
- trade finished student-written texts with another writer and work with a genre list to check that partners have included all the specific information
- listen to a story for evidence of some of the specific information on the genre list and then talk about this
- read a story and apply the specifics of the appropriate genre list to the text

DESCRIPTION

Studying Specimens or Artifacts

what else it looks like

_____ as a _____

what it smells like

_____ as a _____

what it tastes like

_____ as a _____

what it sounds like

____ as a _____

reminds me of

function/use

who uses

where used

why used

Personal Treasure or Family Treasure

treasure info

measurement(s)

age, wear, damage

name, age

color, size, weight

special features

shape, capacity

use or purpose

special story

hand-made or manufactured

present condition

where you got it

how you got it

why you have it

other history

special story

value to owner

monetary value

other value

special care

storage

future of treasure

Personal Work of Art or Well-Known Work of Art

work of art:

date/era of work

artist

description

artist's history

size, color, shape

description

special features

special information

medium/ style

materials used

special techniques

present owner

previous owner(s)

value of piece

history

value to owner

special care

future plans

storage

future

other information

BIOGRAPHY OR AUTOBIOGRAPHY

Human Stories
(to teach, to tell, to learn from)

full name

birth facts/dates

nationality

family background

habits as a child

childhood stories

personality traits

important life event(s)

other events

turn of events

claim to fame

defining moments

setback(s)

accomplishments

contributions

award(s)

memorable quotes

death information

other facts

other special information

concluding remarks

Autobiography: Talents, Abilities, and Interests
(to teach, to tell, to learn from)

name

interest(s) talents

how/why you joined

team/group name

background of interest

where you participate

company you keep

practice/training

preparation

special events equipment/tools

uniforms/special gear

membership

challenges

claim to fame

defining moments

setback(s)

accomplishments

contributions

other info

other special information

concluding remarks

INQUIRY AND EXPLORATION

Burning Questions—*Know, Wonder, Learn Research*
(The specific topic may be a question.)

I know/retell

I wonder …

I learned …

I discovered …

new questions?

other thoughts

conclusions

Where in the World?—*Know, Wonder, Learn, Research*

where in the world?

significance to you

landscape

name, location

special importance

physical features

resources

special sights

special sounds

special features

famous, unique

family/living

special holidays

events/ceremonies

customs

homes

communication

private/public

traditional homes

language

traditional fashion

faith/beliefs

special information

dress

taboos

more special information

little known facts

other

News—*Know, Wonder, Learn Research*

who

what

where

why

when

how

PERSONAL NARRATIVE — MEMOIR

Family Stories/Scary Story
(family teaching, telling and learning)

when I was

who

what we were doing

where

then

what happened

First

I noticed, I had

I felt

Then

I thought

I realized

Suddenly

Next

Then

Finally

I guess

Looking back, I …

When I Was Young Stories
(family teaching, telling and learning)

age/stage

special people/friends

special events/times

special toys/treasures

special songs/music

special TV/movie favorites

special games/sports

special pets/animals

my responsibilities/jobs

favorite place(s)

practices/rituals

favorite clothes/belongings

I knew …

I needed …

I wanted …

I loved/enjoyed

I used to think …

but now I know …

Family Stories (A happy, fun, sad, scary, embarrassing, frustrating, memorable, amazing, special, strange time)

when I was …

how I felt (situation)

where (setting)

that we were doing

where we were

what was happening

First

I noticed, I had

I felt …

I thought

Next

Then

After this

Suddenly,

Finally

I guess

Looking back, I …

"My Memorable Time"
(A happy, fun, sad, scary, embarrassing, frustrating, memorable, amazing, special, strange time)

retell

where I was

situation: background

when

what happened

situation

Next

problem

I thought

I wonder

All of a sudden

I considered

Then …

After that …

I knew …

Finally, I …

I discovered

Personal Story of "My Memorable Day or Night"

On _____ night

I saw

I felt

I could feel

I also felt

I heard

Then I heard

There were (was)

I could smell

I could taste

I really loved the

I will always remember

I will never forget

REVIEW/RESPONSE

The 3 Rs: Retell, Relate, and Reflect

retell (situation)

First, this is about …

Then …

Finally, …

relate

I remember when …

This reminds me of …

I think about …

reflect

I wonder if …

I wonder how …

I wonder why …

This gives me an idea

I think that …

I now know …

I understand …

I now feel …

I realize …

Sharing Stories We Love (teaching, telling and learning)

title, genre

about the author

about the illustrator

date, publisher

audience: who book is for

other books by author

special style of book

Summary: In the beginning …

Then …

Finally …

favorite part(s): I liked …, I thought …

tell about characters

wonderful words

what they say/do

writing style

other noticings

review quotes

other authors with this style

other related books

other noticings

related movies

CHARACTER STUDY

Characterization (teaching, telling and learning)

character

story

description

age, size, shape

special features (eyes, covering)

personality/habits

known for

wanted for

mannerisms

actions

speech

cares about

goals

thoughts

likes/dislikes

characteristics

powerful/weak

content/worried

brave/cowardly

special abilities or powers

worthy of award/praise

harmless/dangerous

worthy of consequences

special contributions

turning points

fate in story

PERSUASIVE WRITING

Standing Your Ground—Opinions

position/opinion

I think …

I believe …

supporting facts

reason

supporting idea

details

facts

examples

other ideas

other thoughts

In the end,

Finally

In conclusion,

It would seem that …

I believe

NARRATIVE

Home Away from Home Stories (teaching, telling and learning)

One day …

character

setting

lives at home

problem

plans to leave

leaves home

goes into the world

dangers escapes

complications

action

emotion

escapes

returns home

ending

Home Adventure Home Stories (teaching, telling and learning)

home: who

setting

situation

adventure: who

setting

situation

problem

decision to go home

home: who

setting

situation

___ used to think …

but now …

he/she knows …

he/she learned …

he/she now understands

Stories (teaching, telling and learning)

situation—who

situation—what

situation—where

Then

After a while

Soon enough

Very soon after

event/problem

problem worsens

situation

resolution

ending

In the end,

Finally,

Then one day,

Bibliography

Anderson, R. C., E. Hiebert, J. A. Scott, and I. A. G. Wilkinson. 1985. *Becoming a Nation of Readers*. Washington, DC: National Institute of Education.

Applebee, A., J. Langer, I. Mullis, A. Latham, and C. Gentile. 1992. *Writing Report Card*. Washington, DC: U.S. National Assessment of Education Progress.

Bereiter, C., and M. Scardamalia. 1991. "Higher Levels of Agency for Children in Knowledge Building: A Challenge for the Design of New Knowledge Media." *The Journal of the Learning Sciences* 1(1): 37–68.

Buis, Kellie. 2004. *Making Words Stick*. Markham, ON: Pembroke.

Brand, Max. 2004. *Word Savvy: Integrating Vocabulary, Spelling and Word Study*. Portland, ME: Stenhouse.

Calkins, Lucy. 1994. *The Art of Teaching Writing*, 2nd Edition. Portsmouth, NH: Heinemann.

Chapman, M. L. 1997. *Weaving Webs of Meaning: Writing in the Elementary School*. Toronto: ITP Nelson.

Cork, Tim. 2007. *Tapping the Iceberg*. Toronto: Bastian Books.

Culham, Ruth. 2003. *6+1 Traits of Writing*. New York: Scholastic.

Daniels, Harvey, and Steve Zemelman. 1988. *A Community of Writers*. Portsmouth, NH: Heinemann.

Graves, Donald. 1989. *Investigating Nonfiction: The Reading/Writing Teacher's Companion*. Portsmouth, NH: Heinemann.

Harvey, Stephanie. 1998. *Nonfiction Matters*. Portland, ME: Stenhouse.

Harvey, Stephanie and Anne Gouduis. 2007. *Strategies that Work, 2nd Edition*. Portland, ME: Stenhouse.

Hillocks, George. 1986. *Research on Written Composition: New Directions for Teaching*. Urbana, IL: National Council of Teachers of English.

Langer, J. 1987. *Language, Literacy, and Culture: Issues of Society and Schooling*. Norwood, NJ: Ablex.

Langer, J. and A. Applebee. 1986. "Reading and Writing Instruction: Toward a Theory of Teaching and Learning." *Review of Research in Education* 13: 171–94.

Mamchure, M. 1990. "But . . . the Curriculum." *Phi Delta Kappan* 71 (April): 634–37.

Murray, Donald. 1999. *Write to Learn*, 6th Edition. Orlando, FL: Harcourt Brace.

Neufeld, G., and G. Mate. 2004. *Hold onto Your Kids*. Toronto: Alfred A. Knopf.

Pedewa, A. 2004. *Classical Teacher*. Atascadero, CA: Institute for Excellence in Writing Seminar.

Rogers, S., J. Ludington, and S. Graham. 1997. *Motivation and Learning: A Teacher's Guide to Building Excitement for Learning and Igniting the Drive for Quality*. Evergreen, CO: Peak Learning Systems.

Ruef, K. 1992. *The Private Eye*. Seattle, WA: The Private Eye Project.

Sullo, Bob. 2007. *Activating the Desire to Learn*. Alexandria, VA: Association for Supervision and Curriculum Development.

Zinsser, William. 1988. *Writing to Learn*. New York: Harper Row.

_____. 1998. *On Writing Well*, 6th Edition. New York: Harper Perennial, HarperCollins.

Index